CAREER GIRLS

by the same author

NAKED and other screenplays
SECRETS & LIES

Career Girls

MIKE LEIGH

faber and faber
LONDON · BOSTON

First published in 1997
by Faber and Faber Limited
3 Queen Square London WC1N 3AU

Phototypeset by Intype London Ltd
Printed in England by Clays Ltd, St Ives plc

A CIP record for this book
is available from the British Library

ISBN 0-571-19404-4

2 4 6 8 10 9 7 5 3 1

CONTENTS

FOREWORD

As old and as wise as you get, or as much as you age, it's still the same old innocent baby you tucked away in there. Run into an old friend years later, and very soon those encrustations of time fall away. Time moves forward and yet stands still simultaneously.

Some time-journeys are longer than others. The ones between thirty and forty, or forty and fifty, are far, far shorter than the long trek from twenty to thirty.

When you're around twenty, you're a seasoned grown-up in many ways, but you haven't quite made it out of your innocent childhood. Most of us at that age are still sorting out the jigsaw puzzle of who we are and who we think we want to be, and how to be who and what we think we should be. Like Hannah and Annie and the others, we're still experimenting and struggling with our identity, even if we don't know or admit it.

But by the time you're thirty you're definitely a grown-up, and you've got it sussed. Or have you?

In *High Hopes*, Cyril says, 'From twenty-five to thirty-five . . . best years of your life, ain't they?'

Perhaps those years also contain one very special, particular Rubicon: the real end of your childhood.

Mike Leigh
London, August 1997

Career Girls was first shown on 29 May 1997 in nine cinemas around New Zealand, and subsequently at the Locarno and Edinburgh Film Festivals of August, 1997.

HANNAH	Katrin Cartlidge
ANNIE	Lynda Steadman
CLAIRE	Kate Byers
RICKY	Mark Benton
MR EVANS	Andy Serkis
ADRIAN	Joe Tucker
RICKY'S NAN	Margo Stanley
LECTURER	Michael Healy

Written and Directed by	Mike Leigh
Produced by	Simon Channing-Williams
Cinematographer	Dick Pope
Editor	Robin Sales
Production and Costume Designer	Eve Stewart
Make-up	Christine Blundell
Original Music	Marianne Jean-Baptiste
	Tony Remy
Sound Recordist	George Richards

A Thin Man Production in association with Matrix Film & Television Partnership for Channel Four.

CAREER GIRLS

In a train. A WOMAN *sits alone at a table, glancing through a magazine. She is respectably dressed, smart but modest. Her hair is short and neat.*

The green countryside speeds past. The woman can't concentrate on the magazine; her mind is elsewhere . . .

A notice-board, headed 'Accommodation' and covered with hand-written notes. A young WOMAN *is copying some information on to a slip of paper. We see that this is the woman in the train, but her hair is dyed red and is in the punk style. And she has a facial skin complaint. She walks away from the notice-board. She is in the corridor of a polytechnic. Students everywhere. She is dressed in black leather jacket, tight leggings and boots. We are seeing her memory, a flashback.*

Back in the train. She smiles. Another memory . . .

It is raining. She arrives at the front door of a drab terrace house. She hesitates. The door opens. Two young women peer round it.

One speaks in an outrageously 'posh' accent:

YOUNG WOMAN: Oh, hello!

Our visitor replies in a Northern accent:

VISITOR: Hallo. Are you, er – Hannah?

HANNAH: It's Hann-*ah*, actually.

VISITOR: Oh, right . . .

HANNAH: And this is Claire. (*She pronounces it 'Clah'.*)

VISITOR: Oh, I'm Annie . . .

HANNAH: Oh! Do come in . . . Annie . . .

ANNIE: Thank you. (*She goes in.*)

HANNAH: (*Broad Cockney accent*) All right? (*She closes the door.*)

In the train ANNIE *smiles as she remembers . . .*

In HANNAH *and* CLAIRE'S *furnished flat.* HANNAH *is using the*

3

carpet-sweeper rigorously. HANNAH *wears jeans, denim jacket, a T-shirt, no make-up and her hair in a pony tail;* CLAIRE *is more decorative – make-up, earrings, lots of bracelets, a yellow plastic slide in her hair. A cassette is playing (The Cure: 'Lovecats').*

HANNAH: I'm just giving Charlie 'is dinner. Oh, sorry! This is
Charlie. And I'm Charlie's Aunt, as in 'Aren't I,
Charlie?' (*To* CHARLIE) You behave yourself.
(*She puts the carpet-sweeper against the wall.*
ANNIE *shakes her asthma inhaler, and uses it.*)
Oh, bloody 'ell, she's on drugs.
ANNIE: It's for me asthma.
HANNAH: (*Asthmatic voice*) Oh, right.
(ANNIE *gets out her cigarettes.*)
ANNIE: Do you mind if I smoke?
CLAIRE: No.
HANNAH: Well, it's a bit kamikaze, innit? (*Karate pose.*) Hai!
CLAIRE: What course are you on?
ANNIE: Psychology.
HANNAH: Oh, bloody 'ell! I'd better get on the couch!
(*She dives onto the couch.* CLAIRE *sits down beside her.*)
ANNIE: Psychoanalysis 'ardly comes into it at all you know.
HANNAH: (*Snooty voice*) Oh, really?
ANNIE: Psychology is actually the scientific study of human
behaviour.
HANNAH: (*Robert De Niro impersonation*) Oh, that's all right
then. 'Cos I'm a dirty rat.
CLAIRE: You can study 'er.
(HANNAH *does a rat pose.*)
ANNIE: So you both do English, then?
CLAIRE: Yeah.
HANNAH: To be or not to be.
CLAIRE: That is the question.
HANNAH: A very good one.
ANNIE: I know what you mean, yeah. (*Pause.*) This is my
favourite band, The Cure.
HANNAH: Oh? It's 'ers, as well (*indicating* CLAIRE).
ANNIE: Really?
CLAIRE: No!
HANNAH: (*Getting up*) So, er . . . what do you think of the old
place – and chips, then?
ANNIE: Nice, yeah – thirty pounds a week inclusive, but, er,
I'm a bit worried 'cos like (*getting out slip of paper*) what

does 'must have G.S.O.H.' mean? 'Cos I don't know if
I've got one, yer see.

(HANNAH *is amusing* CLAIRE *by patting her own cheek in
reference to* ANNIE*'s skin condition.* ANNIE *is unaware of all
this.*)

HANNAH: Oh right. Er, oh that just means, er . . . 'good sense
o' housekeeping'. Don't it?

ANNIE: Oh, right. Well, I have to do a lot of dusting 'cos of
me allergies an' that, so . . .

CLAIRE: It means 'good sense of humour'.

(*An exaggerated mock coughing fit from* HANNAH.)

HANNAH: An analogy to dust! Now what could that be? Er,
God's dandruff, maybe.

CLAIRE: Is that eczema?

ANNIE: No, it's dermatitis.

HANNAH: Well, it's better than determinitis, which is what I've
got. Let's face it.

Back in the train. ANNIE *smiles as she remembers . . .*

She is struggling up the stairs with all her worldly goods. CLAIRE
follows her.

6

CLAIRE: Did you walk?

ANNIE: No, I got a taxi.

(HANNAH *enters the flat from the street and comes up the stairs behind them.*)

CLAIRE: Oh, hello!

(HANNAH *overtakes them both.*)

ANNIE: All right?

(HANNAH *pushes past her and goes into her room and slams the door.* ANNIE *hovers uncomfortably outside her new room.* CLAIRE *comes out of her own room . . .*)

CLAIRE: Go in, Annie, make yourself at home.

HANNAH: (*In her room, shouting*) Bitch! Pervert!

CLAIRE: She's been to see 'er mum.

ANNIE: Oh, right.

(ANNIE *drops her luggage, and sits on the edge of a table.*)

(*In her room,* HANNAH *kicks the door.*)

HANNAH: Never, never! Jesus, she's a fuckin' bitch! I'm never fuckin' going there again – that's it!

(*In her room,* ANNIE *is clearly disturbed by this.*)

And in the train, as she remembers it, she re-lives the pain.

A little later, the train arrives at King's Cross. ANNIE *gets out of the carriage, and closes the door. She walks along the busy platform. She carries a shoulder bag and a parcel wrapped in multicoloured paper. Suddenly she sees* HANNAH *striding towards her. She laughs.* HANNAH *is wearing chic business clothes – a long beige coat over a smart black suit, boots, dyed hair, make-up.*

HANNAH *reaches her. They are both laughing. They stand and look at each other as passengers walk past them.*

ANNIE: Hiya.

HANNAH: Hello!

(*They are still laughing.*)

ANNIE: You look so smart.

HANNAH: Speak for yourself.

ANNIE: Oh, yeah.

HANNAH: No, you do. Let me take this. (*She goes to take* ANNIE*'s shoulder bag.*)

ANNIE: No, it's all right. It's really heavy.

7

(HANNAH *is slightly put out*.)

Er, this is for you – it's er, nothing.

HANNAH: Oh, you shouldn't have bothered. Come on – let me take it.

ANNIE: Oh, all right, then.

(HANNAH *takes the bag. They set off along the platform*.)

HANNAH: Did you get a cuppa tea?

ANNIE: Yeah, and a sarnie. It's only one-and-a-half hours' journey. (*Indicating the parcel*.) Er, it's not much – it's, er, for your flat.

HANNAH: Oh, you didn't need to.

ANNIE: Oh, it's only a last-minute thing, from Doncaster.

HANNAH: The car's not very far, so . . .

ANNIE: Oh? Is it on a meter?

HANNAH: No, it's in the car park.

A few minutes later in the car.

ANNIE: Oh, it feels strange, this.

HANNAH: Yeah, does, doesn' it?

ANNIE: Mm. No, no – I mean London.

HANNAH: Oh, I see. Has it changed much?

ANNIE: It has and it hasn't . . . d'you know what I mean?

HANNAH: I think so.

ANNIE: It all looks the same, but . . . it feels different.

(HANNAH *honks her horn*.)

HANNAH: Stupid tosser!

ANNIE: I'll tell you what is strange, though.

HANNAH: What?

ANNIE: Seein' you drivin'.

HANNAH: (*Laughing*) Well – it's the Company car!

ANNIE: Oh – lucky you! I've got to drive me own jalopy!

HANNAH: Well, you'll get one when you're promoted, won't you?

ANNIE: I hope not to be there much longer.

A flashback . . .

In the girls' flat. HANNAH *takes a paperback from the bookshelf.*

8

HANNAH: Have you read this? (*She displays the front.*) *Withering Heights* by Emily Bront-*eh*?

ANNIE: Yeah, it's great – an' 'er 'ouse is near my 'ouse.

HANNAH: Is it?

ANNIE: Yeah – I've been there.

CLAIRE: Have you?

ANNIE: Yeah – Yorkshire.

HANNAH: Oh, right.

(*Pause.*)

CLAIRE: I've got a question.

HANNAH: Come on, then. (*She holds the book up at* CLAIRE.)

CLAIRE: Ms Brontë, Ms Brontë . . . who will I have sex with next?

(HANNAH *tuts and raises her eyes heavenwards, then she does a 'magic spell' gesture over the book.*)

ANNIE: It's a bit like the *I Ching*, in't it?

HANNAH: Except you don't 'ave to scratch it. (*She opens the book and reads*) 'Himself before. *Erecting* 'imself before'! !

CLAIRE: Yes! !

HANNAH: Yes! ! Well, you'll be all right, then, won't yer?

CLAIRE: 'T's your turn.

HANNAH: No, let 'er 'ave a go!

ANNIE: No . . .

CLAIRE: Go on!

(HANNAH *holds up the book for* ANNIE.)

HANNAH: Come on. Ask Emily your question.

ANNIE: Okay, will I find a feller soon?

HANNAH: No, you've got to say 'Ms Brontë' twice.

ANNIE: Oh, sorry. (*She clears her throat.*) Er, Miss Brontë –

CLAIRE: *Ms* Brontë, *Ms* Brontë!

ANNIE: Oh, okay . . . er, Ms Brontë, Ms Brontë, will I . . . er . . . I will I find a feller soon?

(HANNAH *repeats the hocus-pocus. She opens the book.*)

HANNAH: Wait for it. (*Reads*) 'Must come' ! ! WOW ! ! (CLAIRE *whoops.*) At least he'll know what to do with 'is index finger, won't 'e? (*She does a finger-up nostril gesture in* ANNIE*'s face.*) So, er . . . d'you need like special soap for your, er . . .

ANNIE: Yeh. sometimes, yeh . . .

CLAIRE: Is it catchin'?

ANNIE: No.

HANNAH: 'Cos you do look like you've done the tango with a cheese-grater! If you don't mind my saying so.

(*She launches into a mime of doing the tango with a cheese-grater. After a few moments,* ANNIE *gets up and rushes out of the room. She is distressed.*)

ANNIE: 'Scuse me . . .

(HANNAH *holds her forehead remorsefully.*)

Moments later in the bathroom. ANNIE *is crying.* HANNAH *knocks on the door.*

ANNIE: Yeah? !

HANNAH: (*Outside*) Are you all right?

ANNIE: Yeah.

HANNAH: I was only pissin' about!

ANNIE: I know, I know.

HANNAH: You gotta laugh, though, ain't yer?

ANNIE: Yeah, I'm fine thanks – really.

HANNAH: Well – I'll see you in a minute.

ANNIE: Yeah. (*She wipes her nose. She is still crying.*)

Back to the present. HANNAH*'s small saloon car comes along a leafy London street, and pulls up outside a Victorian house.* HANNAH *and* ANNIE *get out. As* HANNAH *opens the tailgate,* ANNIE *looks around.* HANNAH *removes a work folder and* HANNAH*'s bag.*

HANNAH: Here we are. I'm right at the top.

Chattering, they go up the path and into the house. Moments later, they enter HANNAH*'s flat,* HANNAH *leading the way.*

ANNIE: Oh . . . I'm puffed out. I'm really unfit. (*She closes the door.*)

HANNAH: Here we are, Home Sweet Home. Welcome to my humble abode, and other domestic clichés.

(HANNAH *breezes about the place, getting organised.*)

ANNIE: Oh, it's lovely – it's so bright and cheery. I like the yellow. It's still my favourite colour, you know.

HANNAH: Yeah, I painted it when I moved in.

ANNIE: Primrose.

HANNAH: Looks like piss. I've gone off it now. (*She opens the balcony door.*) Right – let's put the kettle on.

(ANNIE *goes to the balcony and looks out.*)

ANNIE: Gorgeous view. Real surprise, eh? Good morrow, Mr Magpie.

(HANNAH *is filling the kettle. She looks around at* ANNIE.)

Sorry, I'm so superstitious.

HANNAH: Oh, you're allowed to be.

ANNIE: Oh, it's daft, I know. Oh, a fax machine!

HANNAH: Yeah, well I need it for work, really.

ANNIE: Oh, you've got everything.

HANNAH: I wouldn't say that.

(*Pause.*)

Now: what would you like? I've got, er – ordinary tea, herbal teas, or . . . there's filter coffee!

ANNIE: I'd like a coffee. D'you mind?

HANNAH: No, not at all – I'm 'aving one.

ANNIE: Oh, what a great settee – is this from Habitat?

(HANNAH *joins her.*)

HANNAH: No, that's one of my sister's cast-offs, actually; it's a sofa-bed.

ANNIE: Oh, is it?

HANNAH: Why don't you sit down? Let me take this. (*She takes the wrapped gift.*) I'll open it later. (*She puts the gift on her desk.*)

ANNIE: Is that where I'm sleeping?

HANNAH: No – I'm sleeping there. *You're* sleeping in *my* boudoir. Follow me.

(*They go through to* HANNAH*'s bedroom.*)

ANNIE: Oh, you've got a skylight!

HANNAH: Yeah. Bit noisy when it rains.

ANNIE: Good for the stars at night. Romantic.

HANNAH: Now, I've put clean sheets on the bed, and there's a fresh towel . . .

ANNIE: Why can't I sleep in there?

HANNAH: Well, because that mattress is even lower than this one, believe it or not; and I remember what you're like with your allergies. So I thought you'd be better off in here.

ANNIE: Well, as long as I'm not *on* the floor, I don't mind.

HANNAH: Well, whatever, anyway. Er – there's the bathroom, if you want to have a crap. And I'm going to make the coffee.

(*She walks out of the room, leaving* ANNIE *a little lost. We hear* HANNAH's *distant voice . . .*)

It is a flashback . . .

HANNAH *and* ANNIE *are staggering along a street; each is bearing a stack of empty boxes.*

HANNAH: I don't know why we don't just get a coffin, and put everything in that.

ANNIE: I can't hear yer!

HANNAH: I said, I don't know why we just don't get a coffin, and put everything in that!

(*They stop at a front door. This is a place we have not seen before.* HANNAH *puts the key to the lock.*)

ANNIE: Oh, 'urry up – I'm *cold!*

HANNAH: All right – I'm going as fast as I can! Who the fuck d'you think I am? Speedy Gonzalez?

ANNIE: My arms are wrecked.

(*They go into the building. The camera has tracked out and tilts up to reveal that they are living in a flat over a Chinese takeaway.*)

Later, in this same flat, they are sorting through piles of paperback books.

HANNAH: (*Aggressively*) Mine! Mine! Mine! Yours! Mine! Mine! D'you want this? (*she holds up* The Good Pub Guide.)

ANNIE: Yeah, I do.

HANNAH: I thought you might. 'Cos I fuckin' well don't! *Introducing Semiotics*! ! Mine! Mine! Oh, look: *Wuthering Heights*! ! (*She holds up a different edition from the one seen earlier.*) Whey don't you ask Ms Brontë to inform you what the rest of your entire life will consist of?

ANNIE: (*Quietly*) Don't want to.

HANNAH: Go on!

ANNIE: No!

HANNAH: I insist!

ANNIE: No! !

HANNAH: So, you don't want to? Well, that's interesting, 'cos neither do I! !

Later. Close-up on some ceramic coffee-mugs.

ANNIE: Er . . . What will we do with these? There's only five.

HANNAH: We'll chop that one in 'arf.

ANNIE: Tell you what: you take three, an' I'll take two. (*She divides them.*)

HANNAH: (*Re-dividing them*) I know: you have three, and I'll have two, and you can give this one . . . (*she puts a mug on a saucer*) to yer mum!

ANNIE: But what about your mum?

HANNAH: My mum? Will probably smash it in a drunken stupor, wouldn't she? (*She stomps off to continue packing.*) (*Throughout this sequence we have heard The Cure: 'Just One Kiss'.*)

Back to the present. ANNIE *is sitting on the Habitat settee.*

ANNIE: Oh, this is great, Hannah – you're so lucky.

(HANNAH *puts a white chair by the coffee table.*)

HANNAH: I'm thinking of moving, actually.

ANNIE: But why? It's perfect.

HANNAH: I want to buy somewhere.

ANNIE: Really?

HANNAH: Yeah.

ANNIE: Why?

HANNAH: I just think it's a waste of money forkin' out for rent, when it's cheaper payin' off a mortgage. (*She has gone over to the kitchen area and brought back a coffee pot and milk carton, both of which she puts on the table.*)

ANNIE: But it's such a big jump, you know.

HANNAH: But it's not very secure being a tenant, though, is it?

ANNIE: Oh, you're so brave. I couldn't buy on me own.

HANNAH: I couldn't buy with anyone else.

(*She has sugar and biscuits.*)

ANNIE: I want to get somewhere with somebody.

HANNAH: Really? Who?

ANNIE: No, no. I mean – well, you know . . . you never know, my luck might change. I might meet somebody. I've got some money saved up.

HANNAH: Well, I should spend it if I was you. (*She takes some coffee mugs and saucers out of the kitchen cupboard.*) I'm not very good at saving, myself. (*She takes them over to the table.*)

ANNIE: Oh, you still use them!

HANNAH: What?

ANNIE: The cups.

HANNAH: Oh yeah, I've had these for years.

ANNIE: Oh, I don't – I've got cacti in mine, in me bedroom. D'you remember when we bought them?

HANNAH: (*Puzzled*) No.

ANNIE: You know, at the market. You had cystitis.

HANNAH: Oh, that's right. You ended up with two, an' I've got two.

ANNIE: No, you've got two, an' I've got three.

HANNAH: Well, that's not very fair, is it?

(*She pours out the coffee.* ANNIE *is a touch nonplussed. She gets out her asthma inhaler, and proceeds to use it.*)

Still ventilating?

ANNIE: Yeah.

HANNAH: Are you drinkin' milk these days, or . . . ?

ANNIE: Er, no thanks.

HANNAH: Okay. Help yourself to sugar.

ANNIE: Oh, thanks.

(*Tense pause.* HANNAH *gets up and closes the balcony door.*) Oh, go on then – I'm on my holidays. (*She helps herself to some milk.*) Might as well!

HANNAH: Live dangerously! Skin's looking good, anyway.

ANNIE: Oh, yeah – it's cleared up. Finally. (*They sip their coffees.*) I'm afraid I still smoke – d'you mind?

HANNAH: Oh? Er . . . haven't got an ashtray.

ANNIE: Oh, it doesn't matter.

(HANNAH *gets up.*)

HANNAH: Wait a minute. Let's think . . . Oh, I know: we could

use this. (*She empties out the contents of a little pot on the bookcase, and gives it to* ANNIE.) There you go. (*She sits down.* ANNIE *lights up.*) Same old contradiction.

ANNIE: How's work?

HANNAH: Oh, it's been a nightmare today.

ANNIE: Oh!

HANNAH: Yeah, well . . . basically, I've inherited this problem from my predecessor – he was my ex-boss . . . and, er, I warned 'im before 'e left . . . but of course he wasn't 'avin' any of it. So, em, he's gone on to greener pastures, an' I've been left holding the baby.

ANNIE: What's the problem, then!

HANNAH: Well . . . you see, he ordered this whole spring range from a firm, and they didn't deliver by the deadline. So, er, I threatened not to pay them. And now they're giving me all this hassle and shit.

ANNIE: Is it envelopes?

HANNAH: No, no – it's a whole range of stationery.

ANNIE: Problems, eh? I've got them, too, 'cos I want to change me job.

HANNAH: Do you?

ANNIE: Yeah, well, you see, you know, I went into Personnel

15

Management 'cos it's all about dealing with people, you
know, but – I've ended up with this job, you know, sort
of like I spend ninety per cent of my time sort of like
shiftin' paper round a desk.

HANNAH: Yeah, yeah . . .

ANNIE: Anyway, it's not the same since Patsy left.

HANNAH: Who's that?

ANNIE: Oh, she was one of the senior secretaries. She was a
real laugh. She retired last year.

HANNAH: Could you excuse me a moment? (*She gets up, and
goes over to her desk, where she puts on her spectacles.*) I've
just remembered something.

ANNIE: Oh, look at you in your specs.

HANNAH: (*Laughing*) Yeah, I only use them for reading and
writing.

ANNIE: You look so mature.

HANNAH: Well, not too mature I hope.

    (ANNIE *smokes her cigarette, and* HANNAH *finishes writing.*)
Oh, I haven't opened your present, 'ave I?

ANNIE: No.

    (HANNAH *proceeds to open it.*)

HANNAH: Nice paper . . . (*She takes off the paper, and throws it
into the bin. There is a layer of bubble-wrap around the gift.
She removes it.*) That's useful, actually. (*She puts the bubble-
wrap on the desk. The gift is a blue ceramic vase.*) It's great.
Thanks a lot. (*She puts it on the desk.*)

ANNIE: It goes with the room.

HANNAH: It's really lovely, actually.

ANNIE: I must buy you some flowers for it.

HANNAH: Thanks.

    (ANNIE *looks insecure.*)

A flashback . . . ANNIE *and* HANNAH *are sitting on a sofa smoking
a joint. We hear The Cure: 'Let's Go to Bed'.*

HANNAH: Well, we don't 'ave to tell 'er, do we?

ANNIE: No. no. Mum's the word.

HANNAH: Only upset 'er anyway.

ANNIE: Yeah. Right, deal, yeah.

HANNAH: To be honest, I've had enough of 'er.

ANNIE: Know what you mean, yeah.

Now HANNAH *is on the same sofa with* CLAIRE. *They too are sharing a joint. Same Cure number.*

CLAIRE: If we start looking for a flat now, right, we should be able to get hold of the third years – what d'you reckon?

HANNAH: Well . . . I'm not quite sure what I'm doin' next year, actually . . .

CLAIRE: What d'you mean?

HANNAH: (*Garbo voice*) I might want to be alone.

CLAIRE: You wanna live on your own?

HANNAH: Well, a change is as good as a rest. And other duck-billed platitudes. (*Doing a 'quacking duck' with her hand.*)

CLAIRE: Well, that's great for me!

HANNAH: Well, I'm sorry if my life isn't very convenient for you.

CLAIRE: What's Annie doing next year?

HANNAH: I dunno.

And now CLAIRE *is on the self-same sofa with* ANNIE. CLAIRE *is bogeying the joint. Same Cure number again.*

CLAIRE: Because if we start looking now, we should be able to find a place for the two of us, yeah?

ANNIE: I don't know if I can afford it.

CLAIRE: Smaller than this.

ANNIE: No, but I want to go home for the summer – anyway, I don't want to think about it.

CLAIRE: Well, Hannah's not interested. She wants to live by herself.

ANNIE: Really?

CLAIRE: Yeah.

ANNIE: Oh, I see.

Back to the present. HANNAH*'s flat.* ANNIE *picks up some printed sheets of paper. She has a glass of wine in one hand.*

ANNIE: I can't believe it. Two-hundred-and-sixty thousand

pounds. Do people actually pay that sort of money for
a two-bedroomed flat?

(HANNAH *is slicing a cucumber in her kitchen area.*)

HANNAH: Apparently so.

ANNIE: It's a joke.

HANNAH: Well, I certainly couldn't afford it. And even if I
could, I wouldn't want it. I'm just being nosy, really. Seein'
'ow the other 'arf lives. I thought it might be fun for you,
as well. Better than traipsing round Buckin'am Palace
or the Tower o' London . . . And you can always go to the
pictures any time you like in Wakefield, can't you?

ANNIE: Oh yeah, it'll be a giggle.

HANNAH: We'll 'ave to look as though we can spend that sort
of money, as well. So that'll be entertaining.

ANNIE: Oh, no, I couldn't – I'll look like the poor relation.

HANNAH: No, you'll be all right – you could be my financial
adviser.

ANNIE: But what if I say the wrong thing?

HANNAH: I'll end up havin' to buy it, let's face it. I hope you
like this restaurant I've booked for tomorrow night. It's
a bit unusual. You do still eat Chinese don't you? (*She
sips some wine.*)

ANNIE: Oh, I'll eat anything, me. Except mushrooms and
peanuts.

HANNAH: Oh, that's a shame! I've just made mushroom and
peanut pie! Joke!

(ANNIE *laughs and bends down to look at* HANNAH*'s books.*)

ANNIE: Do you still read a lot?

HANNAH: Yeah, quite a lot. Specially when I'm travellin'.

ANNIE: I don't – not 'arf as much as I used to. (*She picks up a
miniature notepad.*) Oh, where d'you get this from – it's
so dinky!

HANNAH: You can have that, if you like.

ANNIE: Oh, no – I couldn't.

HANNAH: No. Go on – it's only a free sample.

ANNIE: Oh?

HANNAH: I get lots of them.

(*She joins* ANNIE.)

19

This is a good one. (*She picks up another pad.*) Looks like paper, feels like leather, and it's made of plastic.
(*She gives it to* ANNIE.)
Put all your secrets in there. Have the bigger version, as well.
(*She puts this one on top of* ANNIE's *pile.*)

ANNIE: Oh . . . no, this is too much.

HANNAH: Don't be silly – what about a folder? (*Gives her a folder.*) There you go!

ANNIE: (*Bemused*) Oh . . . thank you! ! (*She laughs.*)

Later. Evening. HANNAH *and* ANNIE *are eating supper at the coffee table.* ANNIE *sits on the sofa,* HANNAH *in her chair. They are drinking red wine.*

ANNIE: We were in Yates's, er, Wine Lodge in Wakefield . . . and, 'e was already 'alf-pissed, you see, 'cos he'd actually been in there, you know, like, since work with 'is friends – anyway, I stupidly chose this moment to sort of like tell 'im that I didn't want to go out with him any more. And d'you know what 'e said?

HANNAH: No.

ANNIE: 'E said that I'd got the hump with him, right?

HANNAH: Mm-hm.

ANNIE: 'Cos once he'd actually said to me that he didn't ever want to get married. Does that make sense to you?

HANNAH: No.

ANNIE: Here I am, you know, like . . . tryin' to end it with this guy, an' 'e's tellin' me that I want to marry 'im. You know, an' I really didn't – I didn't.

HANNAH: Sounds like a dick'ead to me.

ANNIE: Well, 'e is a dickhead.

HANNAH: How long were you with 'im?

ANNIE: A year and a half.

HANNAH: Oh, I don't know how you put up with it.

ANNIE: Well, I didn't, 'cos I left him, didn't I?

HANNAH: Well, he wouldn't 've lasted a weekend with me. That's my problem. None of them do – I just can't hack it.

ANNIE: Serves me right, for getting involved with a bloody
    drunk.

HANNAH: Yeah, I know what you mean. I've just been involved
    with one o' them.

ANNIE: Oh? Oh, I don't know . . . where are you supposed to
    meet a man, you know, at thirty?

HANNAH: Did you leave your Zimmer frame on the train?

ANNIE: (*Smiling*) Thank you very much – it was lovely.

HANNAH: D'you want some more?

ANNIE: Oh, no, no – I couldn't. (*Pause.*) So how is Thelma
    these days?

HANNAH: Oh, she's still the model of maternity, my mother.

ANNIE: (*Brightly*) Oh?

HANNAH: Swigging two bottles of gin a day, and pukin' up my
    Sunday lunches every week.

ANNIE: Oh, dear.

HANNAH: She's in a right old strop at the moment, actually.

ANNIE: Why's that, then?

HANNAH: Oh, stupidly I told 'er that you were coming down
    for the weekend. And she's been insisting that I bring you
    round.

ANNIE: Well, let's go round. I'd be quite happy to.

HANNAH: No, thank you! I wouldn't wish her on my worst
    enemy, let alone my oldest friend. I wouldn't mind a
    weekend off, anyway. She sends her love.

ANNIE: Oh that's nice. Will you send her mine?

HANNAH: (*Grimly*) Mmm. (*Brightly*) So how's Kathy these
    days? Is she still makin' her own bread?

ANNIE: Oh, yeah, yeah – she's great, yeah.

HANNAH: Fantastic, that bread.

ANNIE: She fancies somebody at work.

HANNAH: Does she?

ANNIE: Mmm, a newcomer. But 'e doesn't work in the
    Housing Department.

HANNAH: Mmmm? ! !

ANNIE: Oh, it's really funny seein' 'er dress up to go in every
    day. But, you know, I really wish that she'd meet
    somebody, you know – 'cos like she's been on 'er own for
    such a long time, you know.

HANNAH: Last time my mother 'ad a lover, I 'ad to call the police.

ANNIE: Did you?

HANNAH: Derek. Tried to break in at three in the morning. Didn't last very long.

ANNIE: No, it's strange. 'Cos if she does, you know, like start goin' out with this feller, I'm worried I – I'll be really jealous, you know?

HANNAH: D'you mean jealous of the bloke or jealous of your mother because she's got a boyfriend and you 'aven't?

ANNIE: Oh, no, no – neither. No, it's – well, it's hard to explain, it's, em . . . well, I'm scared I might . . . lose a part of her. Oh, I know it sounds silly, but . . .

HANNAH: You're more like sisters, you two, really, aren't you?

ANNIE: Mm, I suppose so. Well, that's the main reason why I've got to leave home again, you know, because like, I just depend too much on me mum.

HANNAH: My mum depends too much on me.

ANNIE: I need me independence. 'Cos I've never really had it, you see – not like you, you know, you've got your independence, well all this, you know, an' I really admire that.

HANNAH: Yeah, but I never 'ad a choice, did I? I've 'ad independence rammed down my throat ever since I can remember. And I wouldn't exactly call 'avin' to look after your alcoholic mother all your life independent. You know what I mean? Come on! Lets' get pissed.

ANNIE: (*Laughing*) Why not?

(*She holds up her glass and* HANNAH *tops it up.*)

Later still, HANNAH *opens the door of her bedroom.*

HANNAH: All right?

(ANNIE *is tucked up in bed. She is wearing blue pyjamas.*)

ANNIE: Yeah – great, yeah. It's a real comfy bed, this.

HANNAH: I know.

ANNIE: Are you all right on the sofa?

HANNAH: Yeah. I always sleep in there if I'm ill – watch the telly.

ANNIE: Oh, do you?

HANNAH: Yeah.

ANNIE: Thanks for the dinner tonight.

HANNAH: That's all right . . . I'm not much of a chef, as you know.

ANNIE: Just a shame there isn't time for *me* to cook *you* a meal.

HANNAH: Well, maybe next time . . . whatever. I used to like your cookin', actually.

ANNIE: Oh? ! Do you a pasta, for old time's sake.

HANNAH: Living in the pasta! Bon soir! Salty dreams.

ANNIE: Night-night.

HANNAH: Just give us a shout if you want anything.

ANNIE: Mm-mm.

(HANNAH *closes the door.*)

HANNAH *is lying in bed, thinking. She sighs. She is remembering* . . .

A flashback. ANNIE *is walking along the corridor of their first flat. She is putting on a pair of swimming goggles. She goes into the kitchen.* HANNAH *is opening a tin. She is singing Offenbach's 'Can-Can'.*

HANNAH: Hannah Mills performs open can surgery on a tin of tomatoes.

(ANNIE *gets a knife and starts to cut up an onion.* HANNAH *sees her and roars with laughter.*)

ANNIE: What? ! !

HANNAH: What are you wearing?

ANNIE: What does it look like?

HANNAH: You look like Snoopy dressed as the Red Baron!

ANNIE: Well, I can't 'elp it if they make me cry.

HANNAH: Here, d'you wanna snorkel? (*She waves a rubber sink plunger in* ANNIE*'s face.*)

ANNIE: Don't. (*She takes off the goggles.* HANNAH *puts the plunger down, still laughing uproariously.*)

HANNAH: I'm only joking, right! I'll do it.

ANNIE: No – it's all right.

HANNAH: No! I'll chop the onion, and you open the tin, right?

ANNIE: All right.

HANNAH: It don't make me cry – look!

(*She holds a piece of onion to her eye.*)

ANNIE: Well, it's all right for you. You don't suffer from allergies like I do.

HANNAH: I can't cry. I haven't cried since I was nine years old, actually.

ANNIE: Is that true?

HANNAH: Yeah.

ANNIE: Oh, well, I've been crying ever since I can remember – well, since I were eight, 'cos . . . I don't remember anything before that.

HANNAH: Really? Why's that?

ANNIE: I don't know. It's just, like, one big blank.

HANNAH: (*Mock tragic*) My mum and dad split up when I was eight.

ANNIE: Really?

HANNAH: Yeah.

ANNIE: So did mine!

HANNAH: What, when you were eight?

ANNIE: Yeah, me dad walked out on us when we were eight years old, yeah.
(*She gets a pan from a cupboard.*)

HANNAH: (*Mock tragic*) My dad ran off with another woman.
(ANNIE *lights the gas.*)

ANNIE: So did mine. Coincidence, eh?

HANNAH: Synchronicity.

ANNIE: Yeah, but what is synchronicity, and what's, you know like, er, coincidence? 'Cos like Jung says that synchronicity is when two different things happen at the same time, you know like, one's, er, bein' a normal state, and the other, you know, like, is a psychic one. You know what I mean, like?
(ANNIE *has poured some cooking oil into the pan.*
CLAIRE *comes in the front door and walks upstairs sucking a lollipop.*)

HANNAH: Kitchen synchronicity!
(CLAIRE *enters.*)

CLAIRE: All right?

ANNIE: Hallo!

HANNAH: (*Funny voice*) Good evening!

CLAIRE: What's for tea?

ANNIE: Er . . . spaghetti with tuna.

CLAIRE: I hate tuna!

HANNAH: Well, you don't 'ave to eat it, do yer?
CLAIRE: I told you – I don't like the smell of fish!
ANNIE: Sorry.
HANNAH: Don't 'ave a go at 'er – she can cook what she likes!
CLAIRE: It's all right for her – her room isn't next to the
kitchen, is it?
HANNAH: (*Fists up*) D'you wanna fight?
CLAIRE: Oh don't be childish!
(*She goes out.*)
HANNAH: Kojak! !
CLAIRE: (*Off*) Shut up!
HANNAH: (*One finger*) Swivel! ! Bloody cheek.
ANNIE: Well, I feel really bad now.
HANNAH: Well, don't. We like tuna. Right?
(ANNIE *fries the onions. She is upset.*)

Back to the present. HANNAH *is remembering all this. And in the
other room,* ANNIE *is also awake, remembering . . .*

A flashback. In a tiered lecture theatre ANNIE *is sitting amongst
the other students.*
LECTURER: With the publication of *Beyond the Pleasure
Principle* in 1920, Freud enlarged his first theory of
dreams to cover the recurrent nightmares of shell-shocked
soldiers in the First World War.
(*The door slams. A tubby, scruffy male student with long hair
has entered awkwardly and now makes his way to an empty
place, excusing himself as he squeezes past people.* ANNIE
watches this, and smiles a little. The LECTURER *continues . . .*)
Here, the dreams show the compulsion to repeat, and by
doing so, to try to master actively what was done to the
person as a passive agent of trauma . . .

Back to the present. ANNIE *is still in bed remembering.*

LECTURER'*s voice* . . . 'and in an outline of psychoanalysis' . . .
ANNIE *goes on remembering . . .*

*Another flashback. A black London taxi pulls round the corner
outside the flat over the Chinese takeaway.* HANNAH *and* ANNIE

get out, accompanied by the tubby student with long hair. They unload a quantity of luggage including an old portable television, some bags and a box. ANNIE *pays the taxi, and it drives off. Both the girls get the luggage in through the front door. The student does a lot of talking, but not too much of the moving. At one point* ANNIE *is struggling with a heavy cardboard box tied up with string . . .*

STUDENT: Careful with them – they're deleted.

Inside the front door. HANNAH, ANNIE *and* RICKY *(for that is his name) stagger up the stairs with the luggage. (We hear The Cure: 'The Walk'.)*

RICKY: Er, watch me records, won't you? Er –

ANNIE: Ricky, the bathroom's there, on the left.

RICKY: Er, narrow, these, er, stairs, aren't they, er –?

HANNAH: We seem to manage.

ANNIE: For you, you mean?

    (They reach the top landing.)

HANNAH: Just put them down here.

    (They all do so. RICKY *hitches up his trousers.)*

HANNAH: Right – tea.

ANNIE: Lovely.

    *(*HANNAH *and* ANNIE *go into the living room.)*

RICKY: Er, d'you n – em –

Minutes later, in their living room. ANNIE *is standing by* RICKY.

ANNIE: So, what d'you think, then? Cosy, isn't it?

RICKY: Er, er, I don't like the brown.

HANNAH: What brown? *(She hands out mugs of tea. Same Cure number.)*

RICKY: Er, the walls are brown. The wallpaper, er –

HANNAH: It's not brown. It's maroon. We're marooned.

RICKY: It's, er, brown. Er, the, yeah, carpet's, er, brown, and, er, the, er, lino, it – yeah, maybe, er, if you painted it all er, white, it might 'elp, er, raise, er, spirits.

ANNIE: D'you think so, Ricky?

HANNAH: You reckon you'll be all right sleeping on that thing?

    (She is referring to the sofa. RICKY *comes over to it.)*

RICKY: Er, might be, er a bit small, but, er . . .

HANNAH: It's all relative, innit?

ANNIE: You can put the cushions on the floor and sleep 'ere.

HANNAH: Yeah.

RICKY: Ow!! (*He has sat on the sofa. It is indeed small. He has reacted as though something has hurt his bottom.*)

Oh . . . er, it's er, like wooden, er, ribs, er, stickin' – there's one stickin' up us now.

(*The girls giggle.*)

HANNAH: Well don't brag about it – we'll all want to sit there.

(*The girls sit down.*)

RICKY: Er, me bum wouldn't be 'ere when I was sleepin', er – .

HANNAH: (*Robert De Niro voice*) Instead of a bum. Which is what I am.

ANNIE: Well, it'll have to do . . . until you find somewhere else.

HANNAH: Yeah.

RICKY: Er, er –

ANNIE: What a bastard, eh? Your landlord?

RICKY: I was gonna smack 'im one, but, um . . .

(HANNAH *and* ANNIE *giggle.*)

A pub. HANNAH, ANNIE *and* RICKY *are sitting round a table.*

RICKY: No, see – everybody's got like, er . . . different, er, traits.

ANNIE: That's right, yeah.

RICKY: Like you've got your, er, cardinal traits, an' secondary –

ANNIE: Central and secondary –

HANNAH: I'm having one explanation – I don't need two – I'm not stupid, thank you very much.

RICKY: No, there's like, er, three, er, different, er, groups of, er . . .

HANNAH: Traits.

ANNIE: Yeah.

HANNAH: (*Squeaky voice*) Yeah!

RICKY: Er . . . what do you think your, er, cardinal –

HANNAH: My cardinal trait is . . . what do you think about Margaret Thatcher? Do you think she *will* be assassinated? Or do you think she will carry on *ad nauseam* into the next century? How d'you both feel about that?

ANNIE: I don't know.

HANNAH: That's right, Annie – you don't know. And you don't *care* – let's face it.

RICKY: See, er, Abraham Lincoln's, er, cardinal trait was, er, honesty.

HANNAH: Yeah, and look what 'appened to 'im!

RICKY: Why don't, er, you wanna, er, talk about your cardinal, · er –

HANNAH: 'My Cardinal Trait.' By Hannah Mills. My cardinal trait is . . . generosity.

RICKY: Oh?

ANNIE: That's true, Hannah – she's a very kind person, you know.

HANNAH: Oh, my friend concurs, which is very big of her, I must say!

RICKY: That's like, er, your main, er, drivin' . . .

HANNAH: (*To* RICKY) That's right. And do you happen to have a cardinal trait, by any chance?

RICKY: Er, er . . . see, Annie, I think your, er, cardinal –

HANNAH: Never mind 'er – I'm talkin' to you, monsieur.

RICKY: Mm, er . . . mm, er . . . er, honesty. Er, I, er, tell it like it, er . . .

HANNAH: Now that's that's a porky-pie, isn't it, Mr Ricky,
    Richard – what's your surname?
RICKY: Burton.
ANNIE: Burton. Richard Burton – didn't I tell you.
HANNAH: No.
RICKY: Yeah, it's, er –
HANNAH: You're joking, ain't you?
ANNIE: No, really.
    (HANNAH *chortles*.)
RICKY: I, I don't, er, look like 'im or anything, I –
HANNAH: You can say that again.
RICKY: No, em, me mam used to fancy 'im when –
ANNIE: 'E was lovely.
HANNAH: Well, let's just hope you don't end up like him, then.
RICKY: So, em . . . what do you think your, er, cardinal trait
    is then, Annie?
ANNIE: Well, er . . . I don't know – I don't know, if, er . . .
RICKY: See, er, I think you should, er, look up more. See, you
    always, like seem, er, stressed an' that. Like, your . . .
    your behaviour might be like a cause of your, er . . . scabby
    skin an' that.
HANNAH: Excuse me! Do you think your ample form is
    anything to do with the fact that you stuff your face? Or
    is it just that you're not getting enough sex – maybe?
RICKY: I uh . . . I, er, . . . I d – (*to* ANNIE) it's, er, like your
    dream, isn't it?
HANNAH: What dream?
RICKY: Oh, erm, she 'as, er, this dream about, er, this big, er,
    dark feller in 'er bedroom.
HANNAH: Yer, I know.
ANNIE: Dark figure.
RICKY: With a stick.
ANNIE: We had to describe our dreams in a seminar last term.
HANNAH: Oh, how very honest of you.
RICKY: No, it's, er, interesting.
ANNIE: Anyway, I don't want to talk about this.
RICKY: But if you wanna go and see a therapist or
    something . . .

HANNAH: Er, excuse me – she just said she didn't wanna talk about it, so shut up!

RICKY: You're very aggressive.

HANNAH: So?

RICKY: Well, that might come from insecurity.

HANNAH: Well, we're all insecure, ain't we?

RICKY: No, we're like, we're all, er, like (*he gestures helplessly with both hands*).

HANNAH: What, swimming?

RICKY: No, like, er – we're all the centre of our own . . . like, er, attention.

HANNAH: Well, that's better than being in a detention centre. Which is where I could've ended up, let's face it.

RICKY: No, but like, you know, it's like, coming forward.

HANNAH: Well, it's better than being backward, innit?

RICKY: Well, maybe if you . . . tried and listened . . .

HANNAH: I've been listening to your half-baked psycho-babble all fuckin' evening, and I resent being analysed by two polytechnic second-year psychology students! Thank you! !

(*She gets up and walks out of the pub.*)

RICKY: She's, er . . . not very 'appy.

(RICKY *swigs his lager.* ANNIE, *who is smoking a cigarette, is plainly very upset.*)

A few minutes later ANNIE *and* RICKY *cross the road towards the Chinese takeaway under the flat.*

RICKY: She's like a Type, er, 'A' personality . . . like she might have a heart-attack or summat. Er, d'you fancy, er –

ANNIE: No. No, I don't – sorry.

(*They stop outside the Chinese takeaway.*)

RICKY: I think I'll, er . . .

ANNIE: You'll 'ave to knock. But not too loud – okay?

(ANNIE *goes into the flat,* RICKY *into the takeaway. He is the only customer. He speaks to the owner.*)

RICKY: Er . . . I'll 'ave, er, chips an, er, curry sauce, but can you put on a lot of curry sauce, 'cos last time you didn't . . . put enough on.

31

Up in the flat, ANNIE *and* HANNAH *are sitting in* ANNIE*'s room.*
HANNAH *is reflective.* ANNIE *is crying.*
HANNAH: Sometimes I get the devil in me.
ANNIE: No, you don't.
HANNAH: Yes, I do.
ANNIE: I've never seen you like that before.
HANNAH: Sorry.
ANNIE: I was scared. Ricky's so tactless.
HANNAH: You can say that again.
ANNIE: You know, it's a . . . a real private thing to me that
    dream.
HANNAH: I know what it means.
ANNIE: Do you?
HANNAH: I think so.
ANNIE: I wish I did.
HANNAH: I just don't like being psychoanalysed. That's all.
ANNIE: Yeah. Typical psychology students, eh?
HANNAH: I quite like him, actually. He's sussed, in'e?
ANNIE: Yeah, he's all right.
HANNAH: He fancies you.
ANNIE: What?
HANNAH: (*Squeaky voice*) Yes, 'e does!

ANNIE: Oh, don't be so daft!

HANNAH: (*Robert De Niro voice*) Are you talkin' to me?
   (*Vaguely Robert De Niro fists.*)

Darkness. RICKY *is asleep on the sofa. He is snoring. A shaft of light as the door opens.* HANNAH *comes in and crouches down by him for a moment.*

HANNAH: Oi . . . fatso. Sorry.
   (*Oblivious, he carries on snoring.* HANNAH *leaves.*)

The next evening. The living room. HANNAH *and* ANNIE *are bopping together. The Cure are playing ('The Walk').* RICKY *is sitting on the sofa, watching and commenting.* ANNIE *and* HANNAH *try to persuade him to get up and join them. He resists at first, but then gives in. He soon enters into the spirit of things, and starts whooping and leaping about enthusiastically.* ANNIE *announces that she's 'Fucking pissed! !' The three or them bop together for a while. Then . . .*

HANNAH: All right, I'm goin' to bed now.

ANNIE: Well . . . already?

HANNAH: Yeah. (*She opens the door, and waves at them both.*)
   Goodnight.
   (*As she leaves, she puts her tongue in her cheek.*
   ANNIE *and* RICKY *continue to dance.*
   RICKY *waffles incomprehensibly, and* ANNIE *is drunk.*)

Dawn. The living room. ANNIE *and* RICKY *are sitting side by side on the sofa.* ANNIE *is drunk.*

ANNIE: Okay. (*She clears her throat.*) Ms Brontë, Ms Brontë,
   will I 'ave a fuck soon?

RICKY: Er, um, er . . .

ANNIE: Go on! And close your eyes.
   (*He does so. She waves her hands in his face. He opens the book, points to a word, opens his eyes, and reads.*)

RICKY: Er, er, er . . . it says, er, 'death'.

ANNIE: Oh, great – bloody great!

RICKY: That's, er, symbolic.
   (*She snatches the book from him.*)

ANNIE: It symbolises the bloody death of my sex-life, that's
what. – Right, you 'ave a go.
RICKY: Er, er, Miss Brontë, er –
ANNIE: *Ms* Brontë. *Ms* Brontë. Ms – you know, like multiple
sclerosis, you know, so . . .
RICKY: Er, Miss Brontë, er, er, will I?
(*Pause.*)
ANNIE: Will you what?
RICKY: Er . . . er . . . er, er, er, get a fuck?
ANNIE: Oh, right! Same question – okay. Right, let's see. (*She
opens the book.*) Oh, Ricky . . . it's a blank page.
RICKY: Oh, er, er . . .
ANNIE: Oh, sorry.
RICKY: Er, there's nothing in the rules, or . . .
(*She throws the book down.*)
ANNIE: Oh fuck – it obviously doesn't work when you're pissed!
RICKY: Oh, your, em, receptor-site must be clogged.
ANNIE: Oh . . . (*She puts her hand on his and clasps her head.*)
Oh, Ricky, I feel so dizzy . . .
RICKY: I, er . . .
ANNIE: Oh, I'm gonna have to go to bed.
RICKY: Er, erm, er, I like yer.

ANNIE: Oh, well I like you too, you know, we're mates, you an' I, you know – aren't we? (*She gives him some friendly prods.*)

RICKY: Er, n–, erm, er, I, erm, er, I f–, er, I f–, I fancy you.

ANNIE: Er . . .

RICKY: Er, I, I love you, er, like, er . . .

ANNIE: Oh . . . fuck, Ricky. (*Pause.*) Er . . .

RICKY: Er, I don't, er . . .

ANNIE: I'm sorry, er . . . I think you're lovely. You're really smashin', but, er . . .

RICKY: Er, er . . .

ANNIE: Well . . . you see . . . I've got this problem, er . . . well, it's simple, really – it's just that, er . . . er . . .

RICKY: Er . . .

ANNIE: I'm in love . . .

RICKY: Er . . . er . . .

ANNIE: . . . with someone else.

RICKY: Er . . . er-erm, I – erm, er – I fancy, er, some curry an', er, chips from downstairs.
(*He has got up and is standing in the doorway.*)

ANNIE: They won't be open downstairs.

RICKY: I'll, er, er, get you some sweet and, er, sour chicken – er, balls. I'll . . .
(*He leaves.*)

ANNIE: But, it's twenty-five to seven on a Sunday morning: Ricky!
(*But he has gone.* ANNIE *holds her forehead in pain.*)

Back to the present. ANNIE *lies in the dark in* HANNAH'*s bed, remembering all this. She feels the pain . . .*

Another flashback – the memory continues. We hear HANNAH'*s voice. Daylight hours after* ANNIE'*s incident with* RICKY.
HANNAH *and* ANNIE'*s kitchen area.* ANNIE *is wrapped in her bedding.* HANNAH *is dressed. She is sitting on the kitchen worktop.*

HANNAH: Are you sure you don't fancy 'im?

ANNIE: No, I don't.

HANNAH: But you like him a lot.

ANNIE: Yeah, he's lovely.

35

HANNAH: Why don't you fancy 'im?

ANNIE: Well . . . you know, 'e's a bit . . . plump, in't 'e?
   (HANNAH *jumps down from the worktop.*)

HANNAH: Ah! So it's the way 'e looks, then?

ANNIE: What do you think?

HANNAH: I think that's a bit rich, coming from you.

ANNIE: What d'you mean?

HANNAH: Well, you're always going on about how men don't
   find you attractive, 'cos of your, er . . . (*Gesture indicating*
   ANNIE*'s facial skin problem.*)

ANNIE: Well, I'm not attractive, am I?

HANNAH: I think you're attractive.

ANNIE: You're not a feller.

HANNAH: True.

ANNIE: (*Sighing*) I think I'll go back to bed.

HANNAH: 'E's gonna be tired when 'e gets back in 'e?

ANNIE: I hope 'e's all right.

HANNAH: Oh, yeah. He's probably just jumped off Waterloo
   Bridge.

ANNIE: D'you mind?

HANNAH: All right! ! Only jokin'! !

36

(ANNIE *buries her face in her knees.*)
I'm sure he's hunky-dory!

ANNIE *sits in the lecture theatre. Other students are arriving. She looks worried.*

HANNAH *and* ANNIE *are in the Chinese takeaway. The owner hands* ANNIE *a carrier bag – their order.*
ANNIE: Thanks.
HANNAH: Ta.
　　(*They leave the shop, and go round into the flat, talking as they go . . .*)
ANNIE: I feel so guilty.
HANNAH: Well, we can't hang on to his stuff for ever, can we? Won't be the first time it's 'appened to 'im.
ANNIE: The tutors don't give a fuck, you know.
HANNAH: Probably gone home to his nan's.
ANNIE: Shall I try and get his address off the registrar at college? What d'you think?
HANNAH: Yeah. (*She opens the front door.*)
ANNIE: Then we can write 'im a letter . . . See if 'e's okay.
HANNAH: Good thinking, Watson.
　　(ANNIE *follows* HANNAH *inside.*)
ANNIE: It's elementary.
　　(*She closes the door.*)

A wide, flat road. The sea is in the distance, beneath an expansive sky. The sound of seagulls overhead. On the other side of the road, a man is sweeping the gutter. In the foreground is a street-sign saying West View Terrace. ANNIE *and* HANNAH *appear. They are warmly dressed.* ANNIE *carries a canvas rucksack and is holding a carrier bag.* HANNAH *isn't carrying anything.*
HANNAH: 'E said first left, didn't 'e?
　　(ANNIE *spots West View Terrace.*)
ANNIE: Oh, it's this one.
HANNAH: Oh, yeah.
　　(*They set off down the terrace.*)
Don't forget: if 'e's not there, we'll just say we're passing through.

37

ANNIE: Oh, yeah. Well we don't want to frighten 'is nan, do we?

HANNAH: That's right.

> (*They walk a little distance. Now they are in an alley-way, surrounded by back-yard gates.*)

Is it this one?

ANNIE: That's, er, number five, er . . . Oh, no – it's this one. (*She stops by a bland, functional small house.* HANNAH *goes up to the front door.* ANNIE *holds back.*)

HANNAH: There's no bell. Well, come over 'ere. Don't leave it all to me!

(ANNIE *joins her, reluctantly.* HANNAH *knocks. After a while, a chubby woman in her sixties draws back the lace curtain and looks at the girls. Then she opens the door. She is wearing a blue house-coat. She is* RICKY'S NAN, *i.e. grandmother.*)

RICKY'S NAN: Yes?

ANNIE: Hullo.

HANNAH: Hello. Er, does Ricky live 'ere?

RICKY'S NAN: A-ha. Why?

HANNAH: We're friends of 'is.

RICKY'S NAN: Oh?

ANNIE: Yeah, we're just passing through.

RICKY'S NAN: Oh?

HANNAH: Is 'e in?

RICKY'S NAN: 'E's not in any trouble, is 'e?

HANNAH: No!

ANNIE: No, no, nothing like that, no, we're at college with 'im.

RICKY'S NAN: Oh? (*She opens the door a little more.*) From London?

(*At once*)

{ HANNAH: Yeah.

  ANNIE: Yeah, yeah.

RICKY'S NAN: Oh . . . 'E's gone out.

ANNIE: Oh . . .

HANNAH: D'you know when 'e's gettin' back?

RICKY'S NAN: No, not really.

ANNIE: How is he?

RICKY'S NAN: He's fine.

ANNIE: D'you know where 'e is at all?

RICKY'S NAN: 'E might be along the front, like.

ANNIE: (*To* HANNAH) Shall we go an' look for 'im?

HANNAH: Yeah.

ANNIE: Could you tell him that Annie and Hannah called, please?

RICKY'S NAN: Right.
ANNIE: Okay. Thanks a lot, then.
HANNAH: Yeah, thanks.
ANNIE: Bye.
HANNAH: Bye.

(*They leave.* RICKY'S NAN *watches them go.*)

Back to the present. ANNIE *is still lying awake, remembering all this.*

Remaining in the present, it is the next day. HANNAH*'s car drives towards a block of up-market vulgar luxury penthouse apartments.*

A few minutes later, HANNAH *and* ANNIE *are standing at the entrance to this block, which is called 'The Harbour' – there is a nameplate.* HANNAH *is 'power-dressed', in black suit and coat. She is wearing shades.* ANNIE *is dressed as yesterday, in her beige suede jacket.* HANNAH *holds her car-keys. She taps in a three-digit number. They wait. After a few moments a man's voice crackles through the entry phone. He can obviously see them through a TV surveillance system.*

VOICE: Oh, 'ello. Didn't recognize you with clothes on!
    (HANNAH *and* ANNIE *exchange grins.*)
HANNAH: (*Into entry phone*) Excuse me! Is that Mr Evans?
VOICE: Eh?
HANNAH: Er, we were s'posed to be 'ere at two o'clock.
VOICE: Oh – it's Claudine, innit? (*He laughs.*)
ANNIE: Claudine?
VOICE: Has Andy put you up to this?
HANNAH: Who?
VOICE: I've 'eard all about you! 'Oo's your lovely friend?
HANNAH: Oh, right! Er, I think we're talking at cross-purposes, actually! We were supposed to be 'ere at two o'clock to view the flat, yeah? An', er, Jerry Wall said 'e'd spoken to you.
VOICE: No. No, no, no – that's bollocks.
HANNAH: Well, didn't 'e phone you, then?
VOICE: No, 'e told me tomorrow.
HANNAH: No. 'E definitely said today.

40

(ANNIE *walks away, and speaks at the same time as* HANNAH
and the VOICE.)

ANNIE: Oh, great. Bloody waste of time, this.

VOICE: Er . . .

HANNAH: Oh, well, look . . . just forget it. (*She joins* ANNIE.)

VOICE: Er, no, no – I, I tell you what, darlin', come up.

HANNAH: All right, 'darling'; where shall we 'come'?

VOICE: Eighth floor, turn right. Okay?

HANNAH: (*To* ANNIE) Whadda you think?

    (*The buzzer sounds as the man unlocks the door.*)

ANNIE: Well, yeah.

    (HANNAH *nods, and in they go . . .*)

HANNAH: Is it this way?

VOICE: No, the lift's over here.

HANNAH: Like a bloody hotel, innit?

    (*They disappear amongst the palms.*)

In a glass-panelled lift. HANNAH *is standing by the window, still
wearing her shades. The view is of a long, sloping greenhouse-like
corridor running diagonally up the side of a neighbouring block.*
ANNIE *is facing the door.*

HANNAH: Come on – it's great!

ANNIE: I can't!

HANNAH: You won't fall out.

ANNIE: It doesn't make any difference!

HANNAH: You don't know what you're missing.

ANNIE: I don't care.

HANNAH: See, the reason it slopes is so that when the chickens
    lay the eggs, the eggs can roll down to the bottom. It's
    a giant omelette factory, isn't it?

    (ANNIE *looks round briefly. the doors open and* ANNIE *leaves
    the lift.* HANNAH *takes off her shades, and follows.*)

ANNIE: Oh, thank God for that! (*She disappears to the right.*)

HANNAH: Are you all right?

ANNIE: (*Off*) Now I am, yeah.

HANNAH: (*Turning left*) It's this way, innit?

ANNIE: (*Off*) No, I think it's to the right.

HANNAH: Oh, yeah . . .

    (HANNAH *follows* ANNIE. *The lift doors close.*)

They arrive at the door of the apartment in question. The door is ajar. HANNAH *pushes it a little more open. Nobody can be seen.*

HANNAH: Hello?

(*We hear the* VOICE . . .)

VOICE: All right?

(*He appears in the corridor. He is in his mid-thirties. He wears nothing but a white towelling dressing gown and red leather slippers. He is unshaven, and he has a toothbrush in his mouth.* HANNAH *and* ANNIE *exchange looks. He is* MR EVANS.)

EVANS: Come in, girls.

HANNAH: Look, if this is inconvenient, you know . . .

(*He arrives at the door. He keeps he toothbrush in his mouth.*)

EVANS: Oh, no, no – I was just brushin' my teeth, that's all – come in, come in.

(HANNAH *comes in.*)

Go on – straight up.

(ANNIE *follows, and passes him.*)

ANNIE: Hello.

EVANS: All right?

(*He closes the door. The girls stop at the bottom of a staircase.*)

ANNIE: You've got an upstairs?

EVANS: Yes – er, split level: six hundred square feet each floor.

(*A large amateur mural depicting an idealized naked woman looks down on them from the top of the stairs.*)

HANNAH: So this must be the original art-work Jerry was telling me about.

ANNIE: Lady Godiva.

EVANS: No, that's my ex-girlfriend, that.

HANNAH: Well, at least you 'ave to look up to 'er.

EVANS: Hang on a sec.

(*He disappears into a room. They glance around, cautiously.*)

The kitchen. EVANS *goes to the sink and rinses his teeth.*

EVANS: Fancy a cuppa tea?

HANNAH: Er, no thanks. 'Cos we can't stay long, actually.

ANNIE: No, that's right.

(HANNAH *and* ANNIE *have appeared at the kitchen door. On it hangs a 'naughty' apron, consisting of a drawing of a 'sexy' bodice beneath two three-dimensional oversized plastic breasts.*)

EVANS: How about beer?

HANNAH: No, thank you.

EVANS: Glass o' wine?

ANNIE: Er, no thanks.

(EVANS *opens the fridge.*)

EVANS: I'll open a bottle – come on.

(*He takes out a bottle of wine. The girls exchange amused looks about the apron, and* HANNAH *gives it a little tug.*)

HANNAH: Er, is that a microwave?

(EVANS *is getting a corkscrew out of a drawer.*)

EVANS: Microwave, oven, hob.

HANNAH: So, you are off the breast, then?

(*She works away from the kitchen.* ANNIE *and* EVANS *follow.*)

EVANS: Feel free to look around.

(*They enter the living area: it is large and light, and it overlooks the River Thames.*)

HANNAH: Oh my God, look at this.

ANNIE: Oh, a hammock.

EVANS: Yeah, yeah. (*He nudges it, a huge indoor hammock on a frame.*) Fancy a swing?

ANNIE: No, I'll be sick.

HANNAH: I suppose on a clear day you can see the class struggle from here.

EVANS: Yeah – on a clear day you can see forever, love.

(ANNIE *is looking through a round window.*)

ANNIE: It's like a port-hole.

EVANS: Yeah – it's the ship effect.

ANNIE: Oh?

EVANS: (*Offering cigarette*) Smoke?

ANNIE: Er, no thanks.

(*She walks away. Now* HANNAH *is looking through the round window.* EVANS *joins her.*)

EVANS: Snout?

HANNAH: And what *is* through the round window?

(EVANS *raises the Venetian blind.*)

EVANS: Blinding view. That's er . . . Tower Bridge. Just left of the crane is, er, Big Ben. And over there . . . the City. So what's your name, then?

HANNAH: (*Walking away*) Rumpelstiltskin.

(ANNIE *is looking through a mounted telescope.*)

ANNIE: I like your telescope.

EVANS: Oh, thank you very much.

ANNIE: Good for bird-watching.

44

HANNAH: Is it safe to go out here?

EVANS: Course it is.

(HANNAH *opens a door and steps onto the balcony.* ANNIE *follows.* EVANS *sneaks a peep through his telescope.*)

On the balcony, overlooking the river.

ANNIE: Are you going to buy it, then?

HANNAH: Oh, yeah, definitely.

ANNIE: (*Laughing*) With him thrown in?

HANNAH: Yeah, thrown in the Thames.

(*They lean over the wall, and look down.*)

ANNIE: Oh, no . . . (*She goes inside immediately, passing* EVANS *at the door.*)

EVANS: D'you want the lav, love?

ANNIE: (*Inside*) No – I'm fine.

(EVANS *joins* HANNAH *on the balcony.*)

HANNAH: She's got a touch of the Hitchcocks.

EVANS: You what?

HANNAH: Is that your boat?

(*We see a motor cruiser moored to a jetty beneath the balcony.*)

EVANS: No.

HANNAH: What are the neighbours like?

EVANS: Dunno.

HANNAH: Oh, that's cosy, then, innit?

EVANS: Come and look at this.

(*She follows him to the corner of the balcony, where he points up.*)

Canary Wharf.

(HANNAH *looks up at the Canary Wharf Tower, which is very close.*)

HANNAH: It's a shame they couldn't afford an architect, really, isn't it? So how long have you lived here?

EVANS: Four years.

HANNAH: Oh, really? And why are you getting out?

EVANS: Fancy doing a bit of travelling.

HANNAH: What, with the gypsies?

EVANS: No – get a motorbike. Do Africa. Balloon across the Andes, up the Amazon – that kind of thing.

HANNAH: What do you do?

(*He gestures across the river in the direction of the City, beyond the building works in the foreground.*)

What, crane-driver?

EVANS: No – Futures.

HANNAH: Oh.

EVANS: What are you doing later on?

HANNAH: Nothing that involves you, that's for sure.

(*She walks away. He looks her up and down, then follows.*)

In the living area, a few minutes later. HANNAH *is potting a ball on an American nine-ball pool table.* ANNIE *is looking at a framed photograph of a happy little girl in a sailor suit.*

ANNIE: Who's the little girl?

EVANS: That's my daughter, Tuesday. She was born on a bloody Sunday, but 'er mother's bonkers.

ANNIE: She's really cute.

EVANS: I never see 'er. So – so what d'you two do, then?

(HANNAH *joins them.*)

HANNAH: Oh, er, I'm a pathologist and she's a plastic surgeon, actually.

EVANS: Oh, that's handy.

(*He crosses the room.* HANNAH *and* ANNIE *exchange smirks* EVANS *picks up a joint.*)

EVANS: Fancy a whiff of spliff?

ANNIE: No, thanks.

HANNAH: We don't indulge. So, do you get a lot of dry rot up here?

EVANS: No.

HANNAH: What about rising damp?

EVANS: What, a hundred feet up? Leave it out.

HANNAH: Could be high-rising damp.

EVANS: No, it's double glazed.

HANNAH: Oh, really?

EVANS: Yep. (*He lights the joint, takes a deep drag, comes forward and offers it.*) Sure?

ANNIE: No.

HANNAH: Positive.

ANNIE: Have, er, many people viewed it yet?

EVANS: Well, Jerry's got the keys – whatsisname? Fucking

plonker, 'e was supposed to take a couple of people
round last week. Dunno what 'e's playin' at.

HANNAH: So, are you stickin' at your asking price?

EVANS: This is my point, see. I reckon . . . that we could 'ave
a little coup on the go.

HANNAH: What d'you mean?

EVANS: Well . . . axe the parasite.

HANNAH: Who, Jerry?

EVANS: Yeah. He don't have to know about it. I'll bring down
the asking price. Bosh, it's yours. Sorted.

HANNAH: Sounds brilliant.

ANNIE: How much will you come down by?

EVANS: Well, what're you in the market for?

(*Pause.* ANNIE *looks at* HANNAH.)

HANNAH: You got a couple of bedrooms here, haven't you?

EVANS: Yeah.

HANNAH: Where d'you keep them, then?

EVANS: Downstairs. D'you wanna see them?

HANNAH: Can't wait.

EVANS: Come on down . . .

(*He leads the way.* HANNAH *winks at* ANNIE, *who can hardly
contain herself.*)

Fancy a cognac?

HANNAH: No thank you!

ANNIE: No – she's driving. (*She taps* HANNAH'*s back.*) Aren't
you?

HANNAH: That's right.

(*At the bottom of the stairs,* EVANS *adjusts his crutch and
leads on.*)

EVANS: This is the master . . .

(*He goes into the master bedroom and picks up some clothes
from the floor. The girls stop in the doorway. They both clock
something which plainly doesn't amuse them.*)

HANNAH: I see you've been looking through your family
album.

EVANS: Mm . . . yeah, yeah.

(HANNAH *is referring to a dirty magazine, which is on the
bed. He picks it up, and displays it to the girls.*)

That's my sister, that, God bless 'er.

47

(*He sniggers, and puts down the magazine. The girls are not so amused by this either. However, they soon become amused by him: he stops for a moment, looks at them, and takes a long drag of his joint in a coke-snorting sort of way. Then he proceeds . . .*)

En suite bathroom . . .

(*He goes into the bathroom.* HANNAH *and* ANNIE *move closer to it.*)

Power-shower. There's lots of storage space in 'ere, obviously.

HANNAH: Yeah, okay – thanks very much.

ANNIE: Yeah.

HANNAH: We've gotta go now – we've got another appointment.

ANNIE: Yeah, we 'ave.

(*He follows them down the corridor.*)

EVANS: So are you two lookin' for a place together, then?

ANNIE: No, no.

HANNAH: No, I'm the one who's buyin'.

EVANS: Oh, right, I thought you was, er, geezer birds.

HANNAH: Oh, you wish!

ANNIE: No, we're not.

EVANS: I don't mind, or anything.

HANNAH: Oh, thanks very much!

EVANS: You know – love the life you live, and live the life you love. This is my study.

(*He disappears into another room. The girls head for the front door.*)

HANNAH: Okay, see you, then – thanks very much.

EVANS: Hang on, you haven't seen the other loos yet. (*He dashes into another room.*)

ANNIE: No, it's okay.

EVANS: (*Off*) One . . . two . . . bath as well. Never use 'em. (*He scuttles across to yet another unseen room.*) This is the second bedroom.

(HANNAH *opens the front door, and the girls proceed to leave.*)

HANNAH: Yeah, all right, thanks a lot – 'bye!

EVANS: (*Off*) Where are you going? We haven't started yet!

HANNAH: No, it's okay.

EVANS: (*Off*) Hang on!!

ANNIE: Sorry – 'bye!

(She closes the front door. Outside, in the corridor, they run to the lift.)

HANNAH: Right, come on – let's get out of here.

ANNIE: (*Giggling*) What a bloody nightmare!

HANNAH: I wanted to use the loo, as well.

(Erupting into laughter, they arrive at the lift. HANNAH presses the button.)

What a tosser!!

ANNIE: That flat's gross!

HANNAH: Don't be rude about my future home.

ANNIE: Beg your pardon.

(EVANS rushes out of his flat bearing a bottle of champagne and three glasses.)

EVANS: Fancy a glass of champagne?

HANNAH: No, thanks!

(At this moment, EVANS's front door swings shut.)

EVANS: FUCK IT!!!!

(He rushes towards his flat. HANNAH and ANNIE collapse in uncontrollable mirth. The lift doors open, and they get in.)

HANNAH: Come on, quick! Press the button.

(EVANS reappears at the lift.)

EVANS: Listen, why don't we go downstairs, right? I'll show you round the pool, we'll come back up, okay, and we drink this, yeah?

(The automatic doors close on him, but he starts to force his way into the lift.)

HANNAH: No, thank you! (*She pushes him out.*)

EVANS: You got a problem or something, you fuckin' warped –

(The doors close on him again, and again HANNAH pushes him.) What the fuckin' 'ell is the matter with you?!!

HANNAH: 'Bye!!

EVANS: You got a problem – ?

(The lift doors close finally and conclusively on him, the bottle and the glasses. He screams:

WHAT'S THE FUCKING PROBLEM?!!!

(Renewed uncontrollable laughter from HANNAH and ANNIE. EVANS shouts and kicks the door as the lift sets off.)

SLAGS!!!
(*As the lift descends, the girls laugh uproariously and helplessly.*)

And they are still laughing a little later in HANNAH*'s car, as they drive back across London.*
HANNAH: I just don't believe that.
ANNIE: What an idiot!
HANNAH: 'E was coked out of 'is 'ead, though, wasn't 'e?
ANNIE: Was 'e?
HANNAH: Yeah – course 'e was!
ANNIE: 'Ow – 'ow can you tell?
HANNAH: Oh, bloody 'ell! You Wakefield girls. You're 'alf asleep, in't yer?
ANNIE: I'm so naïve.
HANNAH: When are you movin' back to London?
ANNIE: Oh . . . oh, well – I don't know!
(*Their laughter begins to subside.*)
HANNAH: Oh, dear! Now . . . this next flat we're gonna look at, we're actually meeting the estate agent, Lance . . . no, he sounds like a gentleman. I've spoken to 'im on the phone.

Shortly after this, across the road from a tower block of council flats, the girls get out of the car, and climb the front garden steps of a large Victorian house of the kind that is now often divided into flats.
HANNAH: Oh, it's quite nice, isn't it?
ANNIE: Yeah. Oh, I love these old London houses with the steps. Oh, no, another camera!
(*She is referring to the security camera.*
They laugh.)
HANNAH: You can be Claudine this time, right (*The door buzzes, and clicks open.*) Oh! Lance is in a hurry. (*They go in. They enter an empty hall.*)
Oh, nice hall.
(*A young man of around the girls' age comes out of the ground floor flat. He is wearing a dark suit with shirt and tie, and spectacles.*)

MAN: Hello! – Miss Mills!

HANNAH: *Ms* Mills, actually.

MAN: I do beg your pardon, Ms Mills.

HANNAH: Are you Lance, by any chance?

MAN: No, I'm not Lance.

HANNAH: Oh?!

MAN: Lance is ill – I'm covering for him . . . Adrian Spinks.
> (*He produces a business card from his breast pocket and gives it to* HANNAH.)

HANNAH: (*Snatching it*) Thank you very much.

SPINKS: After you.

HANNAH: Thanks.
> (*She goes into the unfurnished flat, followed by* ANNIE. *They pass down a corridor into a newly decorated empty room.*)
> So what's wrong with Lance, then?

SPINKS: Lance? He went out for a vindaloo last night.

HANNAH: (*Aside, to* ANNIE) Oh, well, spare us the details.
> (*Drily*) It's a very nice white room, isn't it?
> (ANNIE *looks round. She seems to be slightly agitated.*)

ANNIE: Yeah.

HANNAH: Why have you got the shutters closed?

SPINKS: I've just got here – you're my first lot.

HANNAH: Not 'cos you're trying to block out the tower block, then?
> (SPINKS *opens the wooden shutters. Whilst he is doing so,* ANNIE *gestures to* HANNAH, *but* HANNAH *doesn't get whatever* ANNIE *is trying to say. In fact, she goes over to the window.*)

SPINKS: Light up your life.
> (HANNAH *looks out of the window.* SPINKS *circles round the room.*)

HANNAH: It's not very scenic, is it?

ANNIE: Nice big windows.

HANNAH: Yeah, but what can you see through 'em?
> (*She goes over to a fitted wardrobe, opens the door, and looks inside.* ANNIE *moves towards another door.*)

ANNIE: So what's in there?

SPINKS: Take a peek. It's the en suite.
> (*He flicks on the bathroom light.* HANNAH *and* ANNIE *go in.*)

HANNAH: It's not a very large bath, is it?

(*Again* ANNIE *tries to tell* HANNAH *something.* HANNAH *mouths a 'what?'* SPINKS *remains outside the bathroom.*)

SPINKS: You can get two in there.

HANNAH: Yeah, two bars o' soap.

SPINKS: You, er . . . looking for a place together, then?

ANNIE: No. (*She leaves the bathroom and walks past him.*)

SPINKS: Hm. Thought you might be.

(HANNAH *raises her eyes heavenward as she comes out of the bathroom.*)

HANNAH: There's a lot o' cracks in these walls, isn't there?

SPINKS: It's purely cosmetic.

HANNAH: What, you painted them on?

SPINKS: No, it's the weight of the plaster.

HANNAH: So?

SPINKS: It shrinks, it cracks.

HANNAH: Well, yeah – I can see that. It's just not very good, is it?

SPINKS: I agree. You get what you pay for.

HANNAH: Ah! So you haven't got your selling heart where your selling mouth is.

(*She leaves the room.* ANNIE *follows.*)

SPINKS: Honesty is my policy.

(*He follows them.* HANNAH *and* ANNIE *are looking round.*)

HANNAH: So what's in here, then? (*She walks through a doorway.*) Oh. I see. Right. So it's a sort of kitchen breakfast wining dining living dying sort of room, really? (*She moves out of the kitchen into the dining area.* ANNIE *follows.*)

SPINKS: (*Demonstrating*) Fridge-freezer, washer-drier, dishwasher. Save your hands for a rainy day.

HANNAH: I don't use my hands on a rainy day.

ANNIE: Excuse me, did you, um . . did you say your name was Adrian?

SPINKS: Mm-hm. Adrian Spinks. (*He grins.*)

ANNIE: I thought so.

(*She looks at* HANNAH. HANNAH *suddenly looks amazed.*)

SPINKS: That's an original Victorian fireplace . . .

(HANNAH *bursts out laughing.*)

No, it is. Come and 'ave a look. (*He gets down to demonstrate.*) You can have an artificial gas coal fire plumbed in . . . or you can burn your own logs. The choice is yours.

HANNAH: I don't believe it!

SPINKS: Honest.

HANNAH: Oh, my God!

> (ANNIE *and* HANNAH *are both much amused.*
> *And* HANNAH *remembers . . .*)

A flashback. A crowded, noisy, steamy party. Red lighting effects.
The Cure is playing ('The Upstairs Room'). HANNAH *is dancing*
alone. Somewhere behind her is a guy with a Mohican haircut. A
young guy is sitting down swigging a bottle of Newcastle Brown
Ale. It is ADRIAN SPINKS, *without the specs, and wearing an old*
shirt and pullover. He gets up, and sidles up to HANNAH, *who*
has a glass in her hand.

ADRIAN: Ex-squeeze me.

HANNAH: Yeah?

ADRIAN: Are you just a girl that can't say n – ?

HANNAH: NO! ! !

ADRIAN: Thought so. (*He swigs his Newky Brown.*)

HANNAH: This is a party, you know – I don't think much of
your dress sense.

ADRIAN: I thought it was meant to be a funeral – you're
wearing black.

HANNAH: (*Continuing dancing*) Well, I've got funereal disease.

ADRIAN: Will I catch it if I 'ave sex with you?

HANNAH: Well, you won't be, so you won't know, will you?

In HANNAH's *bedroom, that same night.* HANNAH *and* ADRIAN
are very lively. HANNAH *is half undressed, still wearing her*
underwear and an open blouse. ADRIAN *is wearing his T-shirt. He*
is kissing her thigh.

HANNAH: No biting – ow! ! (*He has bitten her. Laughing, she*
tries to fight him off. He does it again. She laughs again.) No,
right – that does it. (*She bites his arm. He leans over to*
reciprocate.) No! !

ADRIAN: Come here. (*He pulls her up to him.*)

HANNAH: Excuse me, I'm a lady.

> (*They kiss passionately.*)

Early morning. HANNAH *is sitting astride* ADRIAN, *who is lying on his back on her bed, wearing a Smiths T-shirt.* HANNAH *is naked.*

HANNAH: Well, come on, then.

ADRIAN: I'm in the passenger seat. You're driving.

HANNAH: Ain't got a gear-stick, have I? (*Hitler pose, Thatcher voice.*) This lady's not for turning!

ADRIAN: D'you fancy breakfast?

HANNAH: 'They also serve 'oo sit and wait!'

ADRIAN: Sausage and egg.

(HANNAH *bends over him, and speaks in his ear.*)

HANNAH: Sausage and two eggs 'd be better. (*She sits up again.*)

ADRIAN: It's getting cold – eat up!

HANNAH: D'you wanna fight? (*She raises clenched fists and does boxing gestures. Then, pointing to her left fist –*) Pacifist.

ADRIAN: I want the toilet. (*He gets out of bed.* HANNAH *sighs.*) And when I get back, young man, we'll have more eats and less talk.

HANNAH: Well, 'hurry up!

(*She gets into the bed and lies down.*)

A few minutes later, ADRIAN *comes out of the toilet. He passes* CLAIRE *who is sitting on the landing, deeply engrossed in a telephone conversation . . .*

CLAIRE: It's just I can't. No, really, I can't. Mum, I've got to get it done.

(ANNIE *is in her room. She is doodling Munch* Scream *faces. We can still hear* CLAIRE. ADRIAN *pokes his head round the door.* ANNIE *is taken by surprise.*)

ANNIE: Oh – hiya.

ADRIAN: Working on a Saturday. Bit keen.

ANNIE: I'm makin' some notes for an essay. I've got as far as The Emotional Responses to Fear.

(CLAIRE *is giggling on the phone.*)

ADRIAN: What's it about, ghosts?

ANNIE: No, it's about the erection of, er –

ADRIAN: Ooh, talkin' dirty to me?

ANNIE: No, the erection of body hair and things like that.

ADRIAN: Are you lookin' for a new erection in life?

(*Pause.*)

ANNIE: Would you like some chocolate?

(ADRIAN *comes into the room.*)

ADRIAN: Very kind o' you. Thank you.

ANNIE: Help yourself.

(*He does so. He is standing by the desk – right next to her.*) Nice boxer shorts. (*They're a 'Peanuts – Charlie Brown' strip cartoon design.*)

ADRIAN: Me ex-girlfriend got them for me.

(HANNAH *comes in, wrapped in her duvet.*)

HANNAH: 'Scuse me . . . are you having a tutorial?

(ADRIAN *speaks with his mouth full.*)

ADRIAN: She was just asking about me ex-girlfriend.

ANNIE: I weren't!

HANNAH: You tryin' to do some work, yeah?

ANNIE: Yes, actually. I am.

HANNAH: Right – come on, Casanova. This isn't a bordello, you know. You can't just walk into every boudoir, and choose a different bint.

(*She returns to her room.* ADRIAN *follows, but stops in the doorway.*)

ADRIAN: (*To* ANNIE) Got to go and feed the world.

(HANNAH *marches back to the landing, and puts her foot on the phone, cutting it off.*)

CLAIRE: Oi! !

HANNAH: Try telegrams! !

CLAIRE: What's your problem? ! !

(*Meanwhile, a charged moment between* ANNIE *and* ADRIAN. *Then he leaves.* CLAIRE *can be heard redialling.*)

Back to the present. Moments later in the empty flat . . .

ANNIE: North London Poly – yeah?

ADRIAN: Yeah . . . ? Were *you* there?

ANNIE: Yeah, we both were.

HANNAH: (*Amused*) You were a BABS,* weren't you?

ADRIAN: Were you BABS?

ANNIE: No, she did English.

ADRIAN: What did you do?

* BABS – Business Administration and Business Studies.

56

ANNIE: Psychology.

ADRIAN: I got a 2:2.

HANNAH: Oh, bully for you.

ADRIAN: Spent too much time in the pub.

ANNIE: I got a 2:2 and didn't spend too much time in the pub.

HANNAH: I got a First and I smoked a lot of dope.

ADRIAN: I had a brilliant time.

ANNIE: Oh? Nice for you.

(*She is not pleased. And she remembers . . .*)

A flashback. In the flat. On the landing. HANNAH *gives* ADRIAN *a scrap of paper.*

HANNAH: The population of China. Good luck trying to get through. 'Cos it's usually engaged.

ADRIAN: Do me a flavour – give me me bus fare?

HANNAH: Yeah, you must be joking!

(ANNIE *passes by with an empty mug.*)

ANNIE: See you, then.

ADRIAN: Lend us forty pence.

HANNAH: No.

ANNIE: What for?

ADRIAN: To get me home, else I'll 'ave to walk.

ANNIE: Oh – yeah.

(HANNAH *leans on the wall between them.*)

HANNAH: No, she will not lend you forty pence.

ANNIE: Why not?

HANNAH: Because we're not a bank, that's why! !

ANNIE: (*To* ADRIAN) Sorry.

(CLAIRE *emerges from the bathroom. She is in her dressing-gown, and has her hair wrapped in a towel, turban-style.*)

CLAIRE: Have you been listening to me !

HANNAH: (*Shouting*) HA – HA! !

CLAIRE: What? ! !

ADRIAN: Lend us forty 'ence.

CLAIRE: What for?

HANNAH: Brain surgery!

CLAIRE: I'm skint. (*She goes to her room.*)

HANNAH: Give us a kiss, then.

(ADRIAN *leans over to kiss her, but she draws away. At this moment* ANNIE *passes them on the way back to her room.*)

ADRIAN: Hey, Annie . . . Don't you reckon she should pay me for use of me fetid stump?

HANNAH: Fuck off! ! (*She pushes him downstairs.*)

ADRIAN: Oh! She likes it rough, she does . . .

HANNAH: OUT! ! !

ADRIAN: 'Cos when I fuck a woman, she stays fucked!

(*He continues down the stairs.* HANNAH *watches him go. The front door slams. She looks at* ANNIE. ANNIE *goes into her room and closes the door.*)

This flashback continues. Another winter's day. HANNAH *and* ANNIE *are wandering round Camden Market. Lots of people around.*

ANNIE: So why d'you think 'e 'asn't phoned, then?

HANNAH: I dunno. Maybe he's lost the number.

ANNIE: Are you bothered?

HANNAH: No. Are you?

ANNIE: No! What's 'e like?

HANNAH: What d'you mean?

ANNIE: You know – in the sack.

HANNAH: He's like a sack of potatoes in the sack.

(*They pass three 'human skulls' on display on a stall selling bizarre artefacts.*)

ANNIE: I hate those things – they give me the creeps.

(*She rushes off.* HANNAH *points to one of the skulls, and addresses the stall-holder.*)

HANNAH: That looks like my mum!

(*The stall-holder is unimpressed.* ANNIE *appears at an adjacent hat-stall.*)

ANNIE: Hey, Hannah! (*She tries on a hat with a large artificial sunflower on it.*) I'm like the Flowerpot Men.

(HANNAH *laughs.* ANNIE *does Flowerpot Men noises.*)

HANNAH: (*Posh voice*) Oh, yarse . . . Lavinia. (*She tries on a large floppy hat and does two-finger peace signs.*)
Peace and joy. Oh yeah, yeah, yeah, yeah.
(*They are both looking in a mirror.*)

ANNIE: That's really nice – it really suits you, you know! Yeah
– Paddington Bear.

Now they are at a T-shirt stall. HANNAH *is holding up a Union
Jack T-shirt, to which she is giving the rude two fingers. Then she
hangs it up.*
ANNIE: Hey, Hannah, look at this! Great – I like the colour!
HANNAH: Yeah – 't's only 50p.
    (*They are looking at identical navy blue T-shirts.*)
ANNIE: D'you think it goes with me 'air?
HANNAH: Makes you look like a carrot, dunnit? (*She holds it
    against herself.*) What d'you reckon?
ANNIE: 'T's nice, yeah.
    (*Together soppy voices and curtseying:*)
{ ANNIE: Twins!!
{ HANNAH: Twins!!
ANNIE: Right, 50p. Great!
HANNAH: D'you think we should get 'em, then?
ANNIE: Definitely, yeah.
HANNAH: All right. Excuse me! ! Where's the geezer?
ANNIE: Don't know.
    (HANNAH *looks round for the stall-holder.*)

More flashback: ADRIAN *is lying on his front on the girls' sofa. He is fully clothed.* HANNAH *appears beside him, and sits on his head.*

HANNAH: (*Funny voice*) And then she sat on my face, constable. (ADRIAN *snores.*) Good morning. Would you like some breakfast? A little fuck-on-toast, maybe? (*She bounces up and down on him a little.*)

ADRIAN: A woman's place is on my face.

HANNAH: Useless!

(*She leaves.* ADRIAN *opens his eyes.*)

Now HANNAH *is scurrying along a street in the pouring rain. She has a bag of chips, which she is eating urgently. She grimaces and shrugs as she goes.*

Meanwhile, ADRIAN *is still lying on the sofa back at the flat, although he is now on his back, wide awake, and only half-dressed. He is listening to* ANNIE, *who is standing against the wall, playing with a blue chiffon scarf. She is very tense.*

ANNIE: (*Sighing*) I've got this, er . . . recurring fantasy about . . . em, well . . . in this fantasy, er . . . (*She bites the scarf.*)

I'm having sex – well, actually, I'm being *forced* to 'ave
sex . . . with somebody. (*Pause.*) And the thing is that
. . . there's a lot o' men, you know . . . watchin' us. (*She
sighs, she looks at him and she clears her throat.*)
ADRIAN: Oh?
ANNIE: Don't get me wrong, it's only a fantasy – it's not reality.
It's a myth that a lot o' men believe, but . . . it can lead
to rape. You know, the idea that . . . a woman means
'yeah', when . . . like, em . . . she means, 'no'.
ADRIAN: I could bring me mates back after five-a-side to watch,
if you want.
(ANNIE *is devastated by this. She covers her face with the
scarf.*)

Back to the present. ANNIE, HANNAH *and* ADRIAN *are crossing
the empty living-room towards a large bay window.*
HANNAH: So what's through the square window?
ADRIAN: Ha! It's a divided garden.
HANNAH: Oh, I'm sorry to hear that.
ADRIAN: The furthest bit belongs to this flat.
HANNAH: Well, it's a bit barren, isn' it?

ADRIAN: You can spice it up with your green fingers.

(HANNAH *laughs mirthlessly.* ANNIE *is still looking out of the window. Pause.*)

HANNAH: You don't recognize us at all, do you?

(ANNIE *turns round.*)

ADRIAN: You're vaguely familiar. (*To* HANNAH) I recognize you . . .

HANNAH: Yeah?

ADRIAN: Yeah . . .

HANNAH: What about her?

ADRIAN: (*To* ANNIE) What's your name?

ANNIE: Annie.

(ADRIAN *thinks for a moment.*)

ADRIAN: No. Sorry.

HANNAH: (*Tersely*) Right. – Where's the second bedroom?

(*She walks out of the room quickly. He follows.*)

ADRIAN: Now there's an offer I can't refuse.

(HANNAH *goes into the second bedroom.*)

HANNAH: You've just lost your commission.

(ADRIAN *stops in the doorway.*)

ADRIAN: Ouch!

(ANNIE *looks out of the window. She remembers . . .*)

A flashback. An empty park. HANNAH *is walking towards* ANNIE *and* ADRIAN, *who are sitting together on a bench with their backs to her.* ADRIAN *has his arm round* ANNIE, *and appears to be kissing her hand. As* HANNAH *gets near them . . .*

ANNIE: Ow! You bloody bit the wrong place!

ADRIAN: Bite's worse than me bark.

(HANNAH *walks round the bench and stands in front of them. She throws some bags of crisps and bottles of soft drink at them.*) Oh – she loves me.

ANNIE: Thank you.

(HANNAH *stands up straight, with one arm sticking straight out horizontally.*)

What's that?

HANNAH: I'm being the right angle . . . in a triangle.

ADRIAN: One-armed bandit.

ANNIE: Are you all right?

HANNAH: Yeah – I'm fine. Have a nice time.

ANNIE: Are you sure you don't want me to come with you?

HANNAH: No, it's all right. It's cool.

(*She turns round and walks away.* ADRIAN *calls after her.*)

ADRIAN: Hannah! I wanted strawberryade!

(HANNAH *gives him the one-fingered rude sign, but she doesn't turn round or stop.*)

ANNIE: You're lucky she got you anything at all.

(ANNIE *watches* HANNAH *disappear.* ADRIAN *puts his arm round her. They kiss for a while. Then* ANNIE *stops . . .*)

So . . . why did you, er – split up with your ex-girlfriend, then?

ADRIAN: 'Cos she wanted to whisk me up the aisle.

ANNIE: Really?

(ADRIAN *looks away.*)

ADRIAN: Yeah. Got sick of 'er cryin' all the time.

ANNIE: Was it 'cos o' her . . or, because you don't like commitment?

ADRIAN: It's a load o' bollocks, all that shit. (*He takes his arm away, and sits up.*)

ANNIE: What?

ADRIAN: Commitment. (*Pause.*) Vagina. Nice place. Wouldn't wanna live there.

(*And he gets up and walks off. Shocked,* ANNIE *watches him go. She starts to cry.*)

Back to the present. HANNAH, ANNIE *and* ADRIAN *come out of the second bedroom. They stop in the hall.*

HANNAH: So how long have you been in a state . . . agent?

ADRIAN: Oh – five, six years . . .

HANNAH: I see you've got a wedding ring.

ADRIAN: (*Chortling*) Yeah, I'm married.

HANNAH: How nice.

ANNIE: How long?

ADRIAN: Second anniversary, coming up.

HANNAH: Got any kiddies?

ADRIAN: I certainly have.

HANNAH: How many? Two point two?

ADRIAN: Just the one – as of yet. (*He takes out his wallet, and opens it, to reveal the snapshot of a pretty little girl with curly hair.*) Laura Jane.

HANNAH: Oh, yes! She's as ugly as you, isn't she?

(HANNAH *and* ADRIAN *laugh.*)

ADRIAN: Yeah, it's her birthday tomorrow. Got to go and pick up the cake.

HANNAH: How old is she?

ADRIAN: One – little jelly-tot! She'll be playing for England by the time I've finished with her.

ANNIE: Oh, I forgot you liked football.

(*Annie walks off.* HANNAH *watches him put away his wallet. Then she follows* ANNIE.)

Outside. The front door opens, and out comes HANNAH, *followed by* ANNIE. ADRIAN *is behind.*

HANNAH: Well, it's a load of crap, really, isn' it?

ADRIAN: No, not my cup of tea, neither.

HANNAH: You know what to do with this. (*She puts his business card in his top pocket.*)

ADRIAN: No, it's for you – keep it for your collection.

(HANNAH *and* ANNIE *set off down the steps.*)

HANNAH: No, thank you!

ADRIAN: Nice to you see again, then.

HANNAH: Yeah – 'bye!

(ADRIAN *goes inside and closes the door.*)

You all right?

ANNIE: Fine, yeah.

(*And they walk away.*)

That evening. In the 'unusual' Chinese restaurant. Contemporary decor. Chinese words in neon. Soft lamps on the tables. Jazz-style piped music. Very full and busy. A waiter serves HANNAH *and* ANNIE.

A few minutes later.

HANNAH: That time in the bedsit was the worst for me. Just after you came down to stay. I was right on the edge.

ANNIE: Yeah.

HANNAH: I actually said to myself, 'You've either got to

change, or you're going to go under.' And if I hadn't got that job in the hardware shop, I'd be in the loony-bin by now.

ANNIE: No, you wouldn't.

HANNAH: Yes, I would. He just let me be myself.

ANNIE: It's funny, but . . . all these memories keep flooding back.

HANNAH: See, I hate looking back.

ANNIE: Yeah, but don't forget, I don't remember my childhood, you know. And that's why remembering's so important to me.

HANNAH: Mm. Who wants a crap memory, though?
(*Pause.* HANNAH *helps herself to some more food.*)

ANNIE: You haven't really changed.

HANNAH: D'you want some more rice?

ANNIE: No, thanks.

HANNAH: I've always envied you, you know.

ANNIE: Oh, don't be so daft.

HANNAH: I have!

ANNIE: Why?

HANNAH: I dunno. I admire your innocence.

ANNIE: What d'you mean?

HANNAH: You're a very . . . sort of . . . trusting person.

ANNIE: I trust people too easily. That's why I get walked over. You see, I envy your ability to stand on your own two feet.

HANNAH: Yeah, but that's just self-protection, innit?

ANNIE: And the way you deal with men.

HANNAH: That's all I ever do is deal with them. I mean, at least you're able to fall in love with them. Even though you are a walking open wound.

(*They laugh gently together.*)

I'm not strong enough to be as vulnerable as you.

ANNIE: But . . . I see that vulnerability as a weakness. You're the strong one.

HANNAH: Well, you see, if we could be a combination, we'd be the perfect woman, wouldn' we? Unfortunately, we can't.

ANNIE: I can't use these chopsticks.

HANNAH: You've changed more than you think, you know.

ANNIE: Oh, yeah? In what way?

HANNAH: Well, you've stopped bumping into things. and you can look me in the eye, can't yer?

ANNIE: Yeah, yeah. D'you know who used to always say that to me?

HANNAH: What?

ANNIE: You know, about looking down all the time.

HANNAH: Who?

ANNIE: Ricky. D'you remember him?

HANNAH: Now there's someone I *have* thought about, you see. As opposed to Adrian. Ricky was sussed.

ANNIE: Oh, yeah – very bright, yeah?

HANNAH: I wonder what happened to him .

ANNIE: I really don't know. Maybe he's a rock star.

HANNAH: Yeah, or a company manager.

ANNIE: He might be as thin as a beanpole.

HANNAH: I don't think so – the amount of curry and chips he used to eat.

ANNIE: Mm, fat chance, eh?

HANNAH: Thin chance. No . . . I haven't thought about Adrian at all.

ANNIE: I don't really want to talk about it, 'cos I'm trying to get over today.

HANNAH: Fair enough.

ANNIE: It's ridiculous, but . . . I haven't stopped thinking about him for the last ten years.

HANNAH: I was really quite hurt by all that, you know.

ANNIE: I knew it – deep down inside I knew that, but why didn't you ever tell me?

HANNAH: Well, because I wasn't in love with him; and I knew you were. So, you know . . . He was a shit.

ANNIE: Oh, yeah, he was a shit. But when you're in love with a bastard, you just can't help yourself. You see, psychologically, I look up to my father – you know, I see him as strong. In spite of everything he's done. But he doesn't respect women, and he's never given me the love that I deserve. And that's why I have this . . . need, you know, to – to crave his respect. And seek his approval. That's obviously why I choose the men I do.

HANNAH: I don't respect my father at all. He's weak. Look what he's done to Thelma. I don't ever want to end up like her – not ever. And when I look at men, all I see . . .

67

is dangerous weakness. I don't want it to be that way. I just can't help it. It makes me feel lonely.
(*She is on the edge of tears. They are both reflective . . .*)

A flashback . . .

HANNAH *takes down a poster of Magritte's* Golconde *(the bowler-hatted men falling through the sky like rain). She pulls off the Blu-Tack. The bookshelves are empty. The room is bare.*

ANNIE *is folding up a wall-drape in her room. This is clearly that moving-out occasion again in the flat over the Chinese takeaway.*

Minutes later, ANNIE *comes out of her room carrying a picture frame.*

ANNIE: Er, Hannah . . .

HANNAH: What?

(ANNIE *stops in* HANNAH*'s doorway.*)

ANNIE: Would you like this for when you find a flat?

HANNAH: No. But you can stick this up your arse, if you like.

(*She holds up a bunch of dried grasses. They both laugh sadly.*
ANNIE *puts down the frame, and hovers in the doorway.*)

ANNIE: It's hard to believe. Four years.

(HANNAH *nods. Moments pass. Then they suddenly embrace, and break out into tears and sobbing.*)

ANNIE: You're crying!

HANNAH: Oh, God! Am I?

(*She detaches herself from the embrace, and smacks her forehead in ironical shock-surprise. They both stand, sad and helpless.*)

Back to the present. In the Chinese restaurant.

ANNIE: (*Smiling*) Here's to us!

(*They clink their wine glasses.*)

HANNAH: The Brunty Sisters! !

ANNIE: Oh, yeah – we always get the –

{ HANNAH: (*Together*) brunt of everything!
  ANNIE: (*Together*) brunt of everything!

ANNIE: (*Continuing*) Oh: I found a photograph of you and I, outside the Brontës' house in Haworth.

HANNAH: Did you?

ANNIE: Oh, yeah, but I forgot to bring it down with me – 'cos I wanted to give it to you.

HANNAH: Oh, that's a shame – I'd 've really liked that.

ANNIE: I know. But I'll send you it.

HANNAH: Thanks. I loved that trip.

ANNIE: Yeah, it was good, yeah.

HANNAH: It was quite a revelation, actually.

ANNIE: How?

HANNAH: Well, just seeing the way you were with your family. You know, everyone being nice to one another. I wasn't used to it.

ANNIE: I remember you kept going off on your own.

HANNAH: Yeah, well I was overwhelmed, really.

ANNIE: Does your mum still favouritize Francesca?

HANNAH: Oh, nothing's changed. Everything Francesca does is brilliant. Everything I do's crap.

ANNIE: It's just not fair, is it?

HANNAH: First it was the mellifluous 'cello; and now it's happy families.

ANNIE: And yet you have always been the one to look after her.

HANNAH: Oh, I know. You're the only person who's ever really appreciated me.

ANNIE: Am I?

HANNAH: Yeah.

ANNIE: You know . . . I've never told you this, but . . . D'you remember all those times I was meant to come to London, and never did?

HANNAH: Yeah . . .

ANNIE: I didn't 'cos . . . I was scared.

HANNAH: What were you scared of?

ANNIE: I was scared that if I set foot in London, I'd never want to leave again. And I didn't want to throw me plans out of the window, you see?

HANNAH: Sounds like you should move on, though, anyway.

ANNIE: Oh, yeah, I'm ready to now, yeah.

HANNAH: Be good if you came back to London, wouldn't it?

ANNIE: Mmm . . . oh, well . . . who knows?

HANNAH: Mmm . . .

(They sip their wine.)

The next day, with the city skyline behind them, HANNAH *and* ANNIE *walk along the empty path of a Central London park. A woman jogger comes up behind them. They turn to look at the metropolitan landscape.*

ANNIE: Oh, look – there's Tottenham Court Road . . .

(The jogger comes past them.)

HANNAH: Hey! Look who this is! I don't believe it!

ANNIE: Is that Claire?

HANNAH: It is, yeah!

(And indeed it is CLAIRE. *She is wearing a baseball cap, a tracksuit, trainers and a Walkman; she looks uncharacteristically untidy, and is quite oblivious to* HANNAH *and* ANNIE.*)*

ANNIE: But she's got no make-up on!

HANNAH: I know! *(She laughs.)*

ANNIE: What a bloody coincidence.

(And they both laugh as CLAIRE *jogs her way towards a lamp-post and a waste-bin on the horizon.)*

A little later, in HANNAH's *car, driving through Inner London.*

ANNIE: What's going on – eh?

HANNAH: I know – it's incredible, isn't it?

ANNIE: The chance of that happening is one in a million. You know, seeing two people like that in the same weekend.

HANNAH: Did you notice where we were standin', as well?

ANNIE: No.

HANNAH: We were at a crossroads, weren't we?

ANNIE: Oh, yeah . . . where the two paths meet.

HANNAH: That's right.

ANNIE: Oh, very symbolic.

HANNAH: Must be something in the air!

ANNIE: Oh, Hannah – look where we are!

HANNAH: Yeah.

ANNIE: Oh, there's that chemist.

   (*Together, joke German accent*)

HANNAH: Hef you got zer right prescription,

ANNIE: jah, jah, jah?

HANNAH: Stupid old fart.

ANNIE: D'you think the flat's still there?

HANNAH: I don't know, actually. I haven't been that way for ages.

ANNIE: Could we, er . . . you know?

HANNAH: What, go and see it?

ANNIE: Yeah.

HANNAH: We've got time before the train, haven't we?

ANNIE: Oh, yeah.

HANNAH: Yeah.

And shortly after this, HANNAH's *car pulls up in the street by the old flat. The girls get out, and stroll towards it.*

HANNAH: Well, we've got a few minutes, anyway.

ANNIE: I feel like my nan.

HANNAH: Why?

ANNIE: Well, every time we went out on a Sunday run, she always had to take us to places where she grew up.

HANNAH: Oh, no! !

ANNIE: Oh, no . . .

71

(The Chinese takeaway is boarded up and covered with fly-posters and graffiti. The place is generally run-down.)

HANNAH: Oh, that's a shame, innit?

ANNIE: Typical, eh? Typical.

HANNAH: Oh, that's sad, that is.

ANNIE: I know, it's terrible.

HANNAH: I wonder what 'appened to 'im?

ANNIE: Oh, he probably retired.

HANNAH: Or died.

ANNIE: Don't!

HANNAH: Well, 'e couldn't have gone back to Hong Kong, could 'e?

ANNIE: Makes me feel so old! Oh, no – look at this!

(She goes over to the side door – the front door to their old flat. The original Georgian door has been replaced by a crude modern flushed one.)

HANNAH: Oh, no! I used to really like that old door!

ANNIE: So did I.

HANNAH: Oh . . . I wonder who lives here now.

ANNIE: Hey – look . . .

HANNAH: What?

(ANNIE now goes up to a contemporary Cure poster (Cure: The 13th). They both laugh.)

ANNIE: They've got a new CD out.

(They both study the poster.)

HANNAH: I haven't listened to them for ages – have you?

ANNIE: Oh, yeah. Now and again, yeah.

HANNAH: *Have* you?

(ANNIE nudges HANNAH: she points to a down-and-out person, who is sitting in the boarded-up doorway of the old takeaway. His head is buried in what looks like a large, cuddly toy. They silently acknowledge him, then discreetly walk round to inspect the front of the building.)

ANNIE: This is my old bedroom, up here.

HANNAH: Yeah. There's mine, look . . .

ANNIE: Oh, yeah.

(They are standing, looking at the building. HANNAH glances at the guy on the doorstep. Suddenly she realizes something.

She nudges ANNIE, *who looks at him. They are both startled.*
ANNIE *turns away.*)
ANNIE: Oh, no! No, I don't believe it!
HANNAH: It's not, is it?
ANNIE: It is, it is.
(*They look at him. It is* RICKY.)
HANNAH: Oh, no, no, no . . . This is weird. This is really weird
    now.
ANNIE: I know – it's too much, isn't it?
RICKY: I, I wanted curry and chips but, erm . . . (*He does his
    characteristic hand-gesture, jabbing his finger in the air. He
    is wearing an old dark suit, and a grubby shirt and tie.*)
HANNAH: Oh, I'm sorry. I mean, a coincidence is one thing,
    you know, but, er, this is a joke, innit?
ANNIE: What are you doin' 'ere?
RICKY: Er . . . open-top bus, er . . .
    (HANNAH *moves towards him.* ANNIE *follows.*)
HANNAH: Ricky . . .
RICKY: Er, Plasticine men . . . (*He makes some incomprehensible
    noises and gestures.*)
ANNIE: Are you all right?
RICKY: Don't patronize me. Where's your scabs?
ANNIE: Oh! I don't know, Ricky – they've gone.
RICKY: Why?
ANNIE: Time. Just time.
RICKY: Just goes . . .
ANNIE: Yeah, it does, yeah.
RICKY: Tickin' . . .
ANNIE: Passin' us by . . .
RICKY: Er, empty . . . Fucking empty! !
    (*Pause.*)
ANNIE: Er . . how come you're 'ere?
RICKY: (*To* ANNIE) On the stage, weren't you? Everybody
    laughing at your shout. (*He makes grunting noises.*) Er,
    pig-faced woman.
HANNAH: Where are you living, Ricky?
RICKY: Hartlepool.
HANNAH: When did you come down to London?
RICKY: Last night . . . er, on the bus.

73

ANNIE: Where d'you stay?

RICKY: I . . . I . . . I Aye aye Carumba! Like, er, Carmen
Miranda. You . . . go . . . er, flyin' . . . in the . . . the sand
. . the, er, desert . . . like, er . . . big calendar. See
stones . . . you can only see them from the sky.
(*Tears well in* ANNIE*'s eyes.* HANNAH *is shocked.*)
Eagle's 'ead. Er, big woman. Blocks. D'you, er . . . wanna
'old me elephant? (*He holds out the large, cuddly toy, which
is indeed a blue-and-white elephant, half-wrapped in a
polythene bag.*)

ANNIE: Er, yeah, okay . . . (*She takes it.* RICKY *laughs.*)

RICKY: It's like, er . ., almost as big as you are.

ANNIE: Who's it for?

RICKY: She, er . . . called me a (*spells*) C.U.N.T.

ANNIE: I never!

RICKY: Not you!

HANNAH: Who?

RICKY: She . . . says I'm not the dad, but I am. 'E's gone to
Dungeness, bastard! ! Like, er . . . nuclear power. He got
a transfer from 'Artlepool. Devil's work. You, er . . . wanna
live for ever?

ANNIE: No.

RICKY: (*To* HANNAH) Eh?

HANNAH: I certainly don't.

ANNIE: We don't, Ricky.
(RICKY *produces what looks like a scrap of paper from his top
pocket, and holds it out to* ANNIE.)
Oh? (*She takes it. It is a torn-off snapshot of a baby.*)
Oh, lovely!

RICKY: Oh, the . . . most beautiful . . .

ANNIE: What's she called?

RICKY: He! ! ! (*He snatches the photo back.*) He's a fuckin' boy!
(*He holds it out.*)

ANNIE: Oh, yeah – sorry. He's lovely!

RICKY: Harry.

HANNAH: He's great.

RICKY: 'E's in 'Astings. (*Laughing*) I'm gonna surprise 'er. She
never answers my letters. Goin' a walk in there – fuck
'er! (*More laughter.* ANNIE *puts down the elephant carefully.*)

74

RICKY: (*To* HANNAH) You wanner 'ave a 'old?

HANNAH: No.

RICKY: Go on!

(*She holds it reluctantly. He laughs gleefully.*)

Oh . . it's, er . . . nice to see yer! !

(*The girls nod in agreement, but they don't say anything.*)

You, er, wanna game o' snooker?

ANNIE: Er, no, thanks – we've got to go.

(RICKY *takes an electronic game out of his bag.*)

RICKY: Oh, it's um, a good game. (*He switches it on. A jingle plays.*)

ANNIE: We don't have time.

HANNAH: She's got to catch a train, Ricky. So we've gotta go – all right? (*She gives him the elephant.*)

RICKY: I'm not a, an idiot.

{ HANNAH: (*Together*) I know . . . I know.
{ ANNIE: (*Together*) No . . . we know you're not.

RICKY: I'm . . . like a idiot savant. Just, er, aven't found any savant yet.

(ANNIE *cries.* HANNAH *laughs, and then becomes sad.*)

HANNAH: Are you hungry, Ricky?

RICKY: 'E did good chips!

ANNIE: Yeah – he did great chips.

RICKY: Are you not, er, gonna invite us up for a cuppa tea, or summat?

HANNAH: Oh . . . we haven't lived here for six years, Ricky!

RICKY: Yeah . . . me nan's dead.

HANNAH: Oh . . .

ANNIE: Oh . . . sorry to hear that.

RICKY: She . . . coughing. (*He demonstrates coughing, graphically.*)

HANNAH: When did that happen, then?

RICKY: Like . . . she like, er, coughed all her life up.

(*Now* HANNAH *is crying a little.*)

ANNIE: D'you live by yourself, then?

RICKY: Mind your business! What do you care?

ANNIE: I do care.

RICKY: No, you don't.

ANNIE: I do.

75

RICKY: You, er, don't think about anybody but yourself.
ANNIE: That is not true!
HANNAH: That's not true, Ricky!
RICKY: Oh, button it, you! You never liked us, anyway!
HANNAH: (*Crying*) I did, actually!
RICKY: Shite! !
ANNIE: I thought a lot about you.
RICKY: You don't think! Selfish. Talk, talk, RABBIT! !
ANNIE: That's not true!
RICKY: Ah, tittle off!
    (*They leave him.*)
    Rancid! ! (*He shouts after them.*) Rancid! Go on – fuck
    yer! ! !
    (*They walk towards the car.* HANNAH *touches* ANNIE.)
    LESBOS! ! !

A flashback . . .

HANNAH *and* ANNIE *are hurrying along a terrace of shops in*
RICKY*'s seaside town.* ANNIE *stops.*
ANNIE: Oh, Hannah – I can't do this!
HANNAH: Oh, don't be stupid – come on!
ANNIE: I'm really nervous.
HANNAH: He'll be dead chuffed we've come all this way.
ANNIE: I don't know what to say to him.
    (*They set off again.* ANNIE*'s bag falls off her shoulder, and
    she puts it back.*)
HANNAH: His nan was all right, wasn't she?
ANNIE: Oh, yeah, she was lovely!
HANNAH: I bet he's right spoilt.
    (*The bag falls off again.*)
ANNIE: Oh, bloody 'ell – this fuckin' bag keeps fallin' off me
    shoulder! !
    (HANNAH *takes the bag.*)
HANNAH: Oh, give it to me, for fuck's sake! You're such a
    moaner, you! !

*Soon after this, they are side by side, leaning over a railing on the
seafront.*

ANNIE: It's great to be by the sea, eh?

HANNAH: It is, actually, innit?

ANNIE: All this fresh air.

HANNAH: Yeah. It's wild.

ANNIE: Eh?

HANNAH: Bit of ozone.

ANNIE: Yeah.

(RICKY *has come out of a gentleman's public lavatory right under where the girls are standing.*)

{ HANNAH: (*Together*) Ricky!!
ANNIE: (*Together*)

(*He turns round and looks up at them.*)

RICKY: What're you doin' up 'ere?

ANNIE: We came to see you.

HANNAH: See if you was all right.

RICKY: I'm, er . . . fine, like, er . . . tip-top, so you don't need to give a toss. (*He walks off.*)

ANNIE: (*Shouting*) Have you heard from college?

RICKY: (*Turning*) Fuck 'em!!

HANNAH: (*Shouting*) What about your stuff?!!

(*They run along the balustrade, and down the steps.*)

HANNAH: (*Running*) That's not very 'ospitable, is it?

ANNIE: (*Running*) No, 'e doesn't seem very 'appy to see us at all.

(*Now* RICKY *is standing by the sea wall. The girls run up to him.*)

HANNAH: Don't be like that.

ANNIE: We were worried about you.

RICKY: Come, er, to 'ave a laugh, 'ave you? Take the piss?

ANNIE: No!

HANNAH: Oh, yeah – seven hours on a coach for a laugh! We're not that desperate!

RICKY: Come to lead us on a bit more, 'ave you?

(ANNIE *rushes off.*)

HANNAH: You've upset 'er now!

RICKY: She's not the only one 'oo's upset!

HANNAH: Well, all right! That's why we've come up 'ere – 'cos we care about you!!

RICKY: Well, er . . . fuck off back where you come from!!

77

HANNAH: Well, fuck you, an' all! ! (*She walks away to join* ANNIE.)
RICKY: (*Shouting*) Well, fuck you! !
HANNAH: I'm sorry we bothered! !
RICKY: (*Violently*) FUCK *YOU*! ! *FUCK* YER! ! !
HANNAH: (*To* ANNIE) Come on . . .
(*They walk away as quickly as possible, as* RICKY *rants in the distance.*)
RICKY: FUCK OFF! ! FUCKING – NOSY PARKER! ! NOSY . . . PARKER! ! !
(HANNAH *and* ANNIE *head towards the town.* RICKY *strides angrily along the empty promenade, as the wild North Sea rages in the distance.*)

Back to the present. In the car, on the way to the station. ANNIE *and* HANNAH *are both tearful.*
HANNAH: It's not fair, is it?
ANNIE: No. I should've got his number.
HANNAH: I shouldn't think he's got a mobile home – let alone a mobile phone. Joke! !
(*But neither is much amused.*)

They walk into King's Cross Station.
ANNIE: What time is it?
HANNAH: It's just gone quarter past.
ANNIE: Which platform is it, I wonder.
HANNAH: Dunno. Is it Platform Three? Let's have a look.
(*They stop and consult a timetable display.*)
Oh, no, that's it, isn't it?
ANNIE: Oh, yeah . . . that's this one.
HANNAH: Yeah, that's right.
(*They set off down the platform. A light trickle of other passengers drift in the same direction.*)
I don't mind saying hello at stations, but I don't like saying goodbye.
ANNIE: I don't like stations. I like trains, though.

Moments later. They arrive at the train, and stop by a carriage.

78

ANNIE: It was really great seeing you.

HANNAH: Yeah, and you.

ANNIE: I'll come again. Soon.

HANNAH: Well, wait till you're invited. (*She laughs.* ANNIE *smiles.*) Got you a little present, actually.

ANNIE: You haven't!

HANNAH: Yes, I have.

ANNIE: You didn't have to!

HANNAH: I know! But . . . you gotta ask me a question first.

ANNIE: What about?

HANNAH: A very important question about your life.

ANNIE: Okay. Er . . .

HANNAH: And you gotta say, 'Ms Mills, Ms Mills', twice. (ANNIE *laughs.*)

ANNIE: Oh, no. Okay, Ms Mills, Ms Mills . . . (*A surge of emotion.*) Will I find true happiness soon?

HANNAH: (*Fanfare*) De-derr! ! ! (*She produces the original copy of* Wuthering Heights, *first seen at the beginning of the film.* ANNIE *smiles.* HANNAH *performs the searching ritual, and lands on a random page.*) 'Pang.' Load o' rubbish! Always was.

ANNIE: (*Laughing emotionally*) Thank you. It's a very special present.

(HANNAH *nods. Now she is overcome with emotion. They both are. Tears are near the surface. A moment passes. Then they hug.*)

HANNAH: See yer.

ANNIE: 'Bye.

(*They separate.*)

ANNIE: Ta-ra.

(HANNAH *walks off.* ANNIE *wipes her eye.* HANNAH *turns round.*)

HANNAH: Let's not leave it six years this time!

ANNIE: No, I won't!

(HANNAH *sets off again.* ANNIE *gets into the train. She leans out of the doorway.*)

Hey, Hannah!

(HANNAH *turns round again.* ANNIE *smiles.*)

D'you think there'll be any more coincidences on the train?

HANNAH: I dunno! Maybe you'll meet the Man o' your Dreams! !

And ANNIE *watches* HANNAH *as she walks off down the platform. A couple of times she turns round and waves in a way that has just a whiff of her old student self.*

ANNIE *looks at the book. Then she picks up her bag and goes into the seating area.*

As the train pulls out, HANNAH *wipes her eye, and continues walking.*